北大版海外汉语教材

CHINA & USA
A Course in Comparison Based on
Comparative Culturology

中美国别文化比较教程

I

舒一兵 编著

图书在版编目（CIP）数据

中美国别文化比较教程 I / 舒一兵编著 . —北京：北京大学出版社，2011.3
（北大版海外汉语教材）
ISBN 978-7-301-18504-9

I . 中… Ⅱ . 舒… Ⅲ . 比较文化－中国、美国－对外汉语教学－教材
Ⅳ . ① G04 ② H195.4

中国版本图书馆CIP数据核字（2011）第013939号

书　　　　名：	中美国别文化比较教程 I
著作责任者：	舒一兵 编著
责 任 编 辑：	宋立文（slwwls@126.com）
标 准 书 号：	ISBN 978-7-301-18504-9/H · 2750
出 版 发 行：	北京大学出版社
地　　　 址：	北京市海淀区成府路205号 100871
网　　　 址：	http://www.pup.cn
电 子 信 箱：	zpup@pup.pku.edu.cn
电　　　 话：	邮购部 62752015　　　　　发行部 62750672
	出版部 62754962　　　　　编辑部 62752028
印 　刷 　者：	北京宏伟双华印刷有限公司
经 　销 　者：	新华书店
	787毫米×1092毫米　16开本　9.75印张　180千字
	2011年3月第1版　2011年3月第1次印刷
印　　　 数：	0001－3000册
定　　　 价：	35.00元（附MP3盘1张）

未经许可，不得以任何方式复制或抄袭本书之部分或全部内容。
版权所有，侵权必究
举报电话：010-62752024　　　电子信箱：fd@pup.pku.edu.cn

前　言

　　选修一门从文化学的角度来解释和比较中国文化和美国文化异同的专题课程，会对更好地掌握中文，了解中国起到十分明显的促进作用，这种作用是其他与中文或中国文化相关的课程取代不了的。作为本书的作者，我真诚希望这个建议能得到认真地考虑。

　　文化作为一个术语，各个历史时期的学者对它的解释是不同的。19世纪，英国哲学家、人类学家爱德华·泰勒将文化定义为："所谓文化或文明乃是包括知识、信仰、艺术、道德、法律、习俗以及包括作为社会成员的个人而获得的其他任何能力、习惯在内的一种综合体。"20世纪以来，人们对于文化概念的阐释日趋精细。美国文化学家克罗伯强调人的行为模式，认为文化包括"行为的模式"和"指导行为的模式"。

　　20世纪80年代以来，中国有关文化的研究，从各个视角界定文化的概念。学者们的基本共识是：文化从最广泛的意义上说，可以包括人的一切生活方式和为满足这些生活方式所创造的事物，以及基于这些方式所形成的心理和行为。无论对于文化的概念如何阐释，归根结底总离不开人的活动与生活方式。人创造了文化，文化又塑造了人；人推进了文化的生成与发展，文化又影响与造就了人的特性。这种研究文化现象或文化体系的科学就叫做文化学。

　　比较文化学是对于不同类型文化进行比较研究的学科。所谓不同类型的文化指的是不同的民族、不同的地域、不同的国家所具有的不同文化传统、文化特性、文化发展史与文化形态等。比较文化学是以比较意识、比较思维方式和比较方法为特征的研究学科，而不是简单的形式比较或比附。

　　文化涉及的对象是人。中国有13亿人。根据人类学家和民族学家的研究，这13亿人中存在着56个民族。其中，汉族的人口最多，因此，其余的民族因人数较少的原因，就被称为"少数民族"，如藏族、维吾尔族、蒙古族、满族等等。虽然他们人数较少，但他们生活的区域却几乎占了中国版图的一半，他们的历史和文化无论在深度上和广度上都影响着中国文化。中国历史上最后的三个朝代，除明朝外，元朝和清朝分别是由蒙古族和满族建立的封建王朝。因此，谈论中国文化时若缺少了少数民族文化，就简直是不可思议的事情。国际著名社会学家、人类学家费孝通博士所提出的中国文化的"多元一体论"，科学而系统地阐述了这一观点。本书的编写也力求以这个理论为首个编写出发点，而不仅仅是围绕着汉族文化。

文化是历史的，也是现代的。有些人理解文化时的一个潜台词就是"历史上、过去的事情"。因此，他们十分注重对传统的研究和介绍，而相比较之下，有些淡化或忽视了对当代的、现实的文化现象的研究。本人认为，当代中国文化，特别是中国改革开放以后的文化，正处于与世界文化相互碰撞、相互融合的一个剧变时期。从未来历史的角度来看，这是最值得研究的一个阶段。我们有幸生活在其中，就更没有理由去忽视其在中国文化研究中的地位了。对现实文化进行比较研究是编写本书的第二个出发点。

在经济全球化的时代，世界上各民族文化的区别界限已呈现出越来越模糊和中和的趋势。我们既要承认"越是民族的，就越是世界的"个性文化，也更应该看到因密切融合而相互渗透的共性文化。文化的对比研究不应只局限在狭义的文学、艺术、民俗等，而是应该放到更广阔的领域去审视，观察比较各国文化因素在教育、经济以及政治上的不同作用。从更宽广的范围着手进行对比研究和现象描述，是编写本书的第三个出发点。

文化是一个民族中全体人民大众创造和拥有的，是由这个民族的文化精英，如这个民族的艺术家、文学家、哲学家、教育家、科学家和宗教圣贤，以及他们的作品和思想所代表的，但民族文化不能简单地等同于精英文化。如果我们的目的是了解和比较这一民族文化的全貌，则更应该去了解这个民族普遍的大众文化，因为精英文化是建立在大众文化的基础上的，没有对大众文化的了解，就谈不上了解精英文化。另外，对精英文化的了解应该是建立在它所属的文化学科基础上的，即只有掌握了对这一文化学科的专业知识，才能够掌握某一精英文化的深邃之处。比如，你只有了解了一个民族普遍的音乐审美取向和大众的演奏、演唱方式，如中国江苏无锡当地的民间小调，才能欣赏音乐大师阿炳的作品，如《二泉映月》的奥妙之处。但这似乎已超出了比较文化学的研究范畴，而属于音乐学这个学科了。与美国不同，中国人口的大多数是农民，中国的农民文化内容丰富，特色鲜明，注重包括农民文化在内的大众文化是编写本书的第四个出发点。

以上四点也表明了本书作者基本的中国文化观。

各位读者需要注意的是，本书不是比较文化学的专著，而是要通过比较文化学的理论和方法去了解中美两国在政治、经济、教育、历史、艺术、民族性格，乃至日常生活方面的异同之处，以提高读者的中文水平，并增进对中国文化及中国人的了解。也正因为这个目的，书中介绍的有关中国文化的信息量要大于有关美国文化的信息量，无论课文还是课后练习，均是如此。作为本书的编者，我猜想学生对美国文化的了解也许多过对中国文化的了解。通过本书，把熟悉的美国文化与仍然陌生的中国文化做一个系统而全面的比较，相信会有助于更容易地了解中国文化。

这套教材共选择了30个文化专题。语法和词汇的安排从易到难。课文中的句型和词汇有很多会与一般中文教科书上的句型和词汇重复，因此选修这门课，也有助于学生中文课的学习。每个课文都附有英文翻译，有些练习和活动也可以用英文完成，这些都会对你有所帮助。

关于本书的具体用法，请参看《使用指南》。

舒一兵
于西雅图

Preface

To select a course which is about commenting and comparing with Chinese culture and American culture will greatly promote understanding Chinese language and culture. This function cannot be replaced by other courses in point of Chinese language and culture. As the author of this book, I honestly hope that my ideas will be considered carefully.

Culture, as a glossary definition, has been commented on differently by scholars in different periods. In the 19th century, British philosopher and anthropologist, Edward Tylor defined the so-called culture or civilization as an integration of knowledge, belief, art, morals, law, convention as well as ability and practice that an individual obtains as a social community member. Since the 20th century, the notion about culture has been explained more precisely. American anthropologist, A.L. Kroeber, explaining the behavior mode of human beings, figures out that culture consists of the behavior mode and the mode of instructing behavior.

Since the 1980's, culture has been defined from different points of view in the related research in China. The consensus of Chinese scholars is that culture, in the most generalized meaning, involves the entire lifestyle of the human being and all the elements of life that aim at satisfying his lifestyle, and mentality and behavior formed from his lifestyle. No matter how one explains the culture, it is impossible to go away from the subject of human activities and lifestyles: humans create culture and culture creates humans; humans advance culture's building and development and culture affects and shapes humans' character. The subject of researching cultural phenomenon and systems is called culturology.

Comparative culturology is the subject of study in comparing various cultural types; the so-called various cultural types refer to the different cultural traditions, characteristics, history and forms of different ethnic groups, regions and countries. Comparative culturology is a subject that relates to characteristics for comparing consciousness, ways of thinking and methodology. It is not a simple formal comparison or analogy.

Culture is about people. There are 1.3 billion people in China. By the research of anthropologists and ethnologists, Chinese people consist of 56 ethnic groups. Thereinto, the population of Chinese Han people is the largest. Due to the smaller population of other ethnic groups, they are named Minorities, such as Tibetan, Uigur, Mongolian and

Manchu. Their living areas cover almost half of China's territory although their population is not the largest. Their history and culture impact Chinese culture either in depth or in extension. The last three dynasties in Chinese history, except Ming, Yuan and Qing are the feudalism dynasties established by Mongolian and Manchu. Therefore, it is unthinkable and unimaginable to discuss Chinese culture without talking about Chinese minorities culture. Dr. Xiaotong Fei, the world famous sociologist and anthropologist, states this view systematically and scientifically by his theory of diversified Chinese cultural factors in one integration. This book is based on and inspired by Dr. Fei's theory and doesn't just address Chinese Han's culture.

Culture is not only historical but modern. Some people understand and study Chinese culture as the things in history and past, so they pay much attention to researching and introducing tradition while neglecting the research in modern and real cultural phenomenon. As the author, I think the modern Chinese culture, especially the Chinese culture after China's reformation and open policy, is in the midst of an upheaval that results in Chinese culture and world culture impacting and compromising one another. In view of the future history, this period is the most worthy of being researched. Fortunately, living in this period, we have no excuse to ignore its status in Chinese culture research. The second intention of this book is to research real and modern culture by comparison.

In the age of economic globalization, the distinguishing finitude of the worldwide national culture presents a trend that becomes more and more ambiguous and neutralized. We should acknowledge either individual culture that is more national, more worldwide, or the common culture that is being penetrated by two or more ethnic groups for close amalgamation. The comparison research in culture should not be only limited in the narrow sense of literature, art, folklore, etc., but should be surveyed in a broader scope to investigate the various functions of how each national cultural factors impact education, economy and politics. To research the comparison and describe phenomenon in a broader scope is the third goal of this book.

The culture is created and possessed by the people of the nation, and is represented by the cultural elite, such as artists, litterateurs, philosophers, educators, scientists and religious oracles, as well as their works and thought. But national culture cannot be equal to national elite culture. If our goal is to understand and compare the overall perspective of the national culture, we should understand the common culture of this nation because elite culture is based on the common culture. Not understanding common culture is not understanding elite culture. On the other hand, to understand a kind of elite culture, one should be prepared to understand the cultural subject which this kind of elite culture belongs to. The core of a kind of elite culture will be understanding nothing other than understanding the special knowledge about the subject. For example, none other than you understand a general musical aesthetic orientation and its popular manner of performance and singing, such as the local chanson in Wuxi, Jiangsu, you will be able to appreciate the music of Master A Bing, for instance, the profundity of his *Two Springs Reflect the Moon (Er Quan Ying Yue)*. But it seems to go beyond the scope of the comparative culturology and belongs to musicology. Differently from the United States, the largest population of China are the peasants; Chinese peasant culture is rich and unique. To pay much attention to popular culture and peasant culture as well is the fourth objective of this book.

The above mentioned four goals of this book also indicate my basic cultural view.

What the readers need to know is this book is not a monograph in comparative culturology; it aims at, by the theory and method of comparative culturology, understanding the difference between the politics, economy, education, history, art, national character, even daily life in China and the United States, to improve readers' ability in Chinese language, and understanding Chinese culture and Chinese people. Just for this target, in the book, the information about Chinese culture is more extensive than the information for the culture of the United States no matter whether in texts and practices behind the texts. As the author, I suspect that the reader's information about American culture may be more than that about Chinese culture. Through this book, comparing the familiar American culture and the unfamiliar Chinese culture systematically and comprehensively will help readers understand Chinese culture more easily.

Thirty cultural topics are focused on in the book. The grammar and words are arranged from the easy to the difficult. Most of the sentence patterns and words in this book are repeated in the textbook of Chinese language art; therefore, this course, will help students in their Chinese language art courses. The English version is attached to each text. Some practices and activities can be done in English; all these will help you.

Regarding how to use this textbook, please refer to *How to Use This Textbook*.

Shu Yibing
Seattle

使用指南

这是一部通过比较文化学的方法，将中国文化学习和汉语习得结合起来，利用短小的课文和大量而形式多样的训练，引导汉语学习者了解中国文化，并掌握一定汉语技能的教科书，是对主干汉语教材的一个有益补充。

一、本书简介

1. 课文字数与内容

本教材分上下两册，共30课。课文分中国和美国两个部分。从第一课到第十课，课文约有汉字500个左右；从第十一课到第二十课，课文约有汉字600个左右；从第二十一课到第三十课，课文约有汉字700个左右。

三十个课文在内容上可分为六个单元。每个单元的大致内容如下：

第一单元：从第一课到第五课，主要介绍和比较中美两国的国家概况；

第二单元：从第六课到第十课，主要介绍和对比两国人民的日常生活；

第三单元：从第十一课到第十五课，主要介绍和对比中美两国人民的休闲娱乐；

第四单元：从第十六课到第二十课，主要介绍和比较两国的教育；

第五单元：从第二十一课到第二十五课，主要介绍和比较两国的政治和社会差异；

第六单元：从第二十六课到第三十课，主要介绍和比较两国的经济、文化及民族性格。

2. 词汇和专有名词

词汇包括课文中的基本生词和短语。专有名词单列。

3. 练习

练习有判断、选择、问答以及资料搜集、探索、讨论和报告七个内容。前三项内容主要是考查对课文的阅读理解情况；而后四项内容的主要目的是引导、帮助读者扩展某一专题下的有关中国文化的知识量，并对某一中国文化专题进行分析、讨论和演讲，以增强对问题的理解和研究的兴趣。有些活动的设计是学生之间，或师生之间互动性的，需要学生集体完成，或通过教师的指导和参与完成。

4. 信息链接

信息链接的主要功能是帮助读者更好地理解课文，顺利完成练习，并增加关于中国文化的知识量。所推荐的网站中，有些是中文的，如果你阅读时有困难，可以借助汉英词典。这里建议读者使用翻译软件"金山词霸http://www.iciba.com/"里的屏幕取词功能，它十分快捷方便，并且可免费使用。其他的翻译软件也可使用，如：

http://cidian.youdao.com/
http://www.tigernt.com/cedict.shtml
http://www.mandarintools.com/worddict.html
http://dictionary.reverso.net/english-chinese/
http://www.lexiconer.com/ceresult.php

5. 英语译文

每课的最后部分是课文的英语译文，它能帮助学生正确理解汉语课文的意思。

汉语水平尚未提高的学生也可以在读完英语译文后，用英语做一些有关中国文化方面的练习和活动，这样依然有助于读者理解中国文化，并提高学习汉语的兴趣和能力。

6. 答案

针对每课练习中的"判断"和"选择"两题，给出参考答案。

二、使用方法

1. 作为学生，如何确定本教材是否合适？

（1）阅读课文目录及部分课文的英语译文，看看其大部分内容是不是平时感兴趣的文化专题，并考虑你是否具备关于这些专题所涉及的美国文化方面的知识。

（2）翻阅每课的词汇表，与目前学习的汉语教材的词汇表相比较，看看重合率是否在40%以上。

（3）作为汉语初学者，请看看是否对课文内容、练习感兴趣。请注意：你的中文水平并不是选修本课程的障碍，因为，本课程以了解中国文化为主要目的，学习中文为次要目的，是从比较文化学的角度辅助学生学习中文的。

（4）向教师咨询。

（5）试听一周的课，然后再做决定。

2. 建议的教学安排

（1）课时安排：每课一般用3～5课时完成。建议的课时安排是，课文部分需1～2课时，练习和活动部分需2～3课时。

（2）要求学生预习。

（3）作为课后作业，要求学生完成大部分练习及活动项目。

（4）每课至少安排一次报告或讨论。

3. 如何处理课文与练习之间的关系

可以发现，在一课中，课文比较短小简单，而练习量却比较大。这是因为，作者认为即使课文文字再长，内容再丰富，也难以把一个文化现象讲得全面周到，还反而会影响学生对中国文化的知识扩展和独立研究，并难以从中美两国的文化比较中得出自己的结论。因此，课文只是一个简单的"开场白"，或"启发点"，起引导作用。

另有一点需要着重说明，练习中关于中国文化的成分大于关于美国文化的成分，这是因为本书编写目的是为需要学习中文和了解中国文化的学生服务的，从情理上来讲，这些学生对美国文化的了解应该远远多于对中国文化的了解。

除"判断"、"选择"和"问答"之外，其余的练习用中文或英文完成均可。

4. 如需进一步了解或讨论本书使用方法，请函至本书作者：
edmondshu@yahoo.com

How to Use This Textbook

This is a textbook that integrates learning about Chinese culture and acquiring Chinese language skills by the method of comparative culturology. As a salutary supplement for the Chinese language art textbook the reader is using, it applies short and easy-reading texts as well as mass and multiform exercises to induce Chinese language beginners to understand Chinese culture and learn Chinese language.

1. Introduction

A. Chinese character count and content of the text

This two-volume book consists of 30 lessons. There are two parts addressing China and the USA in each text. There are about 500 Chinese characters in each text from Lesson 1 to Lesson 10, about 600 Chinese characters in each text from Lesson 11 to Lesson 20, and about 700 Chinese characters in each text from Lesson 21 to Lesson 30.

By the contents, the thirty texts can be divided into 6 units; the overall content of each unit is the following:

The first unit, from Lesson 1 to Lesson 5, covers the overview of China and the USA;
The second unit, from Lesson 6 to Lesson 10, covers the lifestyle of both peoples;
The third unit, from Lesson 11 to Lesson 15, covers entertainment;
The fourth unit, from Lesson 16 to Lesson 20, covers education;
The fifth unit, from Lesson 21 to Lesson 25, covers the social and political differences;
The sixth unit, from Lesson 26 to Lesson 30, covers the economy, culture and national character.

B. Words and phrases

Words include the basic words and phrases in the text. The proper nouns are listed separately.

C. Practice

The practice consists of True-False Questions, Multiple Choice, Short Answer Questions and Data Collection, Exploration, Discussion as well as Presentation. The first three practice aim at evaluating reader's reading comprehension, and the final four practice aim at directing and helping readers to know more about Chinese culture regarding to a certain topic, and then do some research, discussion and presentation about it. It will improve the understanding of the topic and increasing the interest in it. Some pracitce must be performed in an interaction of students, or, between teacher(s) and students. They are required to be completed by a group or through the instruction and participation of teacher(s).

D. Information link

The key function of the information link is to help readers understand texts better, complete the practice successfully, and expand knowledge of Chinese culture. Some of the recommended web-sites are in Chinese. If you find it difficult to read, you can look up new words in a Chinese-English dictionary. The function of the open cursor translator of www.iciba.com is recommended because it is fast and free. The other translator softwares can be used as well, such as:

http://cidian.youdao.com/
http://www.tigernt.com/cedict.shtml
http://www.mandarintools.com/worddict.html
http://dictionary.reverso.net/english-chinese/
http://www.lexiconer.com/ceresult.php

E. English version of the text

The last part of each lesson is an English Version of the Text; it is helpful to understand the Chinese text precisely. The readers who are in lower level of Chinese language proficiency can do some practice and activities about Chinese culture after reading the Engllsh version, and increase their interest and ability in learning the language.

F. Keys to exercises

The keys to True-False Questions and Multiple Choice of each lesson are given for reference.

2. How to use this textbook

A. As a student, how to know this textbook is a right selection for you?

a. Read the text catalog and some English version to see if most of the contents are the cultural topics you are interested in and if you have background information about the relevant American culture.

b. Skim the Vocabulary behind each text and compare it with your textbook to see if the superposition is above 40%.

c. If you are just a Chinese language beginner, please see if you are interested in the text and practice. Please notice that your Chinese language level is not a barrier to select this course, because the main target of this book is to understand Chinese culture, and the sub-target is to learn Chinese language. It assists students in learning Chinese by comparative culturology.

d. Talk about it with your teacher.

e. Decide after a 1-week trial.

B. The suggested teaching arrangement

a. Hour: each lesson can be completed in 3-5 hours. The suggested breakup of hours is 1-2 hour(s) for text, 2-3 hours for practice and activities.

b. Students are required to make a preparation.

c. As the homework, students are required to complete the majority of practice and activities.

d. A presentation or a discussion for each lesson should be held at least once each week.

3. How to manage the text, practice and activity

It can be seen that each text is short and the practice is long. This is because the author thinks even if the text would be longer, and its content would be richer, it is hard to explain a cultural phenomenon roundly and entirely, and on the contrary, it will even interfere with students' knowledge extension and independent research on Chinese culture and they would have difficulty reaching conclusions of their own by comparing cultures between China and the USA. Therefore, the text is only a prologue or an inspiration, playing a role of guide.

Another point which needs to be stressed is that the component about Chinese culture in practice is longer than the one about American culture because the book is for the students who need to learn Chinese language art and understand Chinese culture. If you are not at the precondition, you have to spend more time learning American culture.

Except for the True-False Questions, Multiple Choice and Short Answer Questions in practice, the rest can be completed in Chinese or English.

4. If you need more information or discussion on how to use this book, please contact the author via edmondshu@yahoo.com.

目录 CONTENTS

第 一 课　山水　　　　　　　　　　　　　　　　　　　　　　1
Lesson 1　　Mountains and Waters

第 二 课　城市　　　　　　　　　　　　　　　　　　　　　　10
Lesson 2　　Cities

第 三 课　王小明和汤姆·史密斯　　　　　　　　　　　　　　19
Lesson 3　　Wang Xiaoming and Tom Smith

第 四 课　故宫和白宫　　　　　　　　　　　　　　　　　　　27
Lesson 4　　The Palace Museum and the White House

第 五 课　你好！　　　　　　　　　　　　　　　　　　　　　35
Lesson 5　　Hello!

第 六 课　厨房　　　　　　　　　　　　　　　　　　　　　　42
Lesson 6　　Kitchen

第 七 课　城里和农村的住房　　　　　　　　　　　　　　　　53
Lesson 7　　Houses in City and Countryside

第 八 课　自行车和汽车　　　　　　　　　　　　　　　　　　61
Lesson 8　　Bicycle and Automobile

第 九 课　工资单与税　　　　　　　　　　　　　　　　　　　69
Lesson 9　　Payroll and Tax

第 十 课　挂号　　　　　　　　　　　　　　　　　　　　　　79
Lesson 10　Registration for Hospital Treatment

第十一课　餐厅里的热闹与安静　　　　　　　　　　　　　　87
Lesson 11　The Noise and the Quietness in Restaurants

第十二课	茶馆和星巴克	96
Lesson 12	Teahouse and Starbucks	

第十三课	乒乓球和棒球	105
Lesson 13	Pingpong and Baseball	

第十四课	出发	115
Lesson 14	Let's Go!	

第十五课	商店趣事	124
Lesson 15	Funny Stories in the Store	

部分练习答案 — 132
Keys to Exercises

词汇总表 — 135
Vocabulary

第一课 山水
Shānshuǐ
Lesson 1 Mountains and Waters

中国的东部和东南部濒临太平洋，是平原和丘陵地带。北部、西北和西南部是沙漠和高山。东部低，西部高，在地图上从东向西看中国，就好像一级一级向上的楼梯一样，而每一节楼梯上的风景是不同的。珠穆朗玛峰 (Zhūmùlǎngmǎ Fēng, the Mt. Qomolangma) 在中国西部，它有8844.43米①高，是世界上最高的山峰。

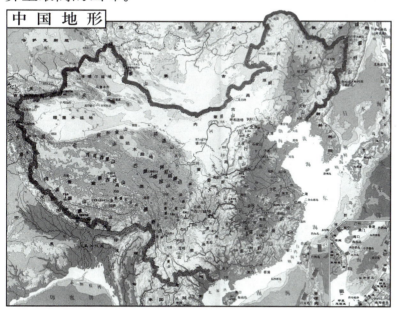

中国有许多河流。黄河和长江是中国最大的两条河流。东北部的黑龙江 (Hēilóng Jiāng, the Heilongjiang River)，中部的淮河 (Huái Hé, the

---

① 国家测绘局，2005年。State Bureau of Surveying and Mapping, 2005.

Huaihe River)，南部的珠江 (Zhū Jiāng, the Pearl River)，西南部的澜沧江(Láncāng Jiāng, the Lancangjiang River) 都是很大的河流。从北京到杭州的大运河是世界上最长、最古老的人工河。中国的湖泊也很多，比如青海湖 (Qīnghǎi Hú, the Qinghai Lake)、太湖 (Tài Hú, the Taihu Lake) 都很广阔，很美丽。

美国的东部、西部分别濒临大西洋和太平洋，南部濒临墨西哥湾，北部与加拿大土地相连，西南部与墨西哥土地相连。美国的东部和中部是广阔的低地和平原，西部是盆地和草原，西部海岸地区又是低地和平原。美国也是东部低，西部高，但她看上去更像是一块大大的绿色地毯。

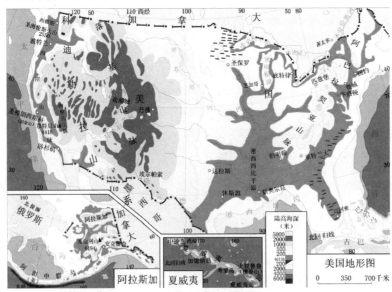

密西西比河 (Mìxīxībǐ Hé, the Mississippi) 在美国中部，从北向南流到墨西哥湾。科罗拉多河 (Kēluólāduō Hé, the Colorado River) 和哥伦比亚河

(Gēlúnbǐyà Hé, the Columbia River) 在美国西部，流入太平洋。中北部的五大湖区是世界上最大的湖区。东部的阿巴拉契亚山脉 (Ābālāqìyà Shānmài, the Appalachian Mountains)，西部的洛基山脉 (Luòjī Shānmài, the Rocky Mountains) 和内华达山脉 (Nèihuádá Shānmài, the Sierra Nevada) 对美国的气候和地理的影响很大。

词汇 Vocabulary

部 bù	part, partial		湾 wān	gulf
濒临 bīnlín	to be close to, border on		相连 xiānglián	link to
平原 píngyuán	plain		草原 cǎoyuán	grassland
丘陵 qiūlíng	hill		海岸 hǎi'àn	seashore, coast
沙漠 shāmò	desert		地区 dìqū	area, region
级 jí	degree, level, step		地毯 dìtǎn	carpet
楼梯 lóutī	stair		流 liú	flow, stream
风景 fēngjǐng	scenery, view		山脉 shānmài	mountains, range
山峰 shānfēng	peak		气候 qìhòu	climate
运河 yùnhé	canal		地理 dìlǐ	geography
广阔 guǎngkuò	vast, large		影响 yǐngxiǎng	affect, impact, influence
美丽 měilì	beautiful			

专有名词 Proper Nouns

太平洋 Tàipíng Yáng	Pacific Ocean
黄河 Huáng Hé	the Yellow River
长江 Cháng Jiāng	the Changjiang River, the Yangtse River
北京 Běijīng	capital of China
杭州 Hángzhōu	a city of China

大运河 Dàyùn Hé	the Great Canal
大西洋 Dàxī Yáng	Atlantic Ocean
墨西哥 Mòxīgē	Mexico
加拿大 Jiānádà	Canada

课文理解 Understanding of the Text

一、判断 True-false questions

1. 中国东部、东南部频临大西洋。　　　　　　　　　　　　□ 对　□ 错
2. 中国东部低，西部高，好像一级一级向上的楼梯一样。　□ 对　□ 错
3. 珠穆朗玛峰是中国最高的山峰，但不是世界最高峰。　　□ 对　□ 错
4. 淮河在中国的南部，澜沧江在中国的北部。　　　　　　□ 对　□ 错
5. 美国五大湖区是世界上最大的湖区。　　　　　　　　　□ 对　□ 错

二、选择 Multiple choice

1. 中国的两条大河是_____和_____。

　　A. 黄河　　　　B. 哥伦比亚河　　　C. 科罗拉多河　　　D. 长江

2. 8844.43应该怎么读？_____。

　　A. 八十八百四十四点四十三　　　　B. 八和八百四十四点四三
　　C. 八千八百四十四点四三　　　　　D. 八百四十八和四点四三

3. 中国的大运河是从_____到_____。

   A. 北京　　　　　　　　B. 纽约 (Niǔyuē, New York)

   C. 杭州　　　　　　　　D. 旧金山 (Jiùjīnshān, San Francisco)

4. _____和_____是中国的两个大湖。

   A. 黑龙江　　B. 太湖　　　　C. 珠江　　　　D. 青海湖

5. 美国的东部、西部分别濒临_____和太平洋。

   A. 印度洋　　B. 密西西比河　　C. 大西洋　　　D. 哥伦比亚河

三、问答 Short answer questions

1. 中国的地形特点是什么？What is the feature of landscape of China?

   _____
   _____
   _____

2. 中国有哪些大河、大湖？What big rivers and big lakes does China have?

   _____
   _____
   _____

信息链接 Information Link

http://www.dlpd.com/
http://www.geochina.net/
http://cn.bing.com/ditu/
http://maps.google.com/
http://www.maps.com/
http://www.nationalgeographic.com/

http://chinadatacenter.org/chinageography/
http://afe.easia.columbia.edu/china/geog/maps.htm
http://www.jhdyh.net/
http://www.chinapage.com/canal.html

资料搜集 Data Collection

三峡大坝 The Three Gorges Dam

汉语拼音_____

2008 中国汶川 5·12 大地震
The earthquake of Wenchuan, Sichuan Province, May 12, 2008

汉语拼音_____

塔克拉玛干沙漠 Taklimakan Desert

汉语拼音_____

第一课 山水
Lesson 1 Mountains and Waters

桂林山水 Guilin's Scenery, Guangxi

汉语拼音_____

拓展活动
Extention

一、探索 Exploration

请在地图上标出下列地点：
Mark the following locations on the map:

黄河　长江　大运河
珠穆朗玛峰　北京
杭州　青海湖

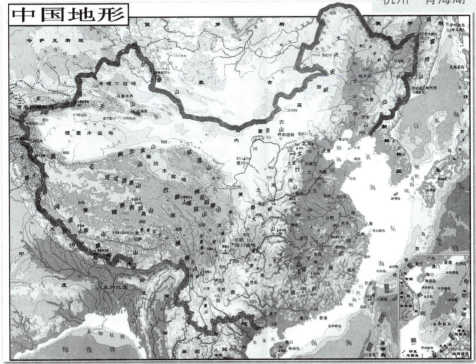

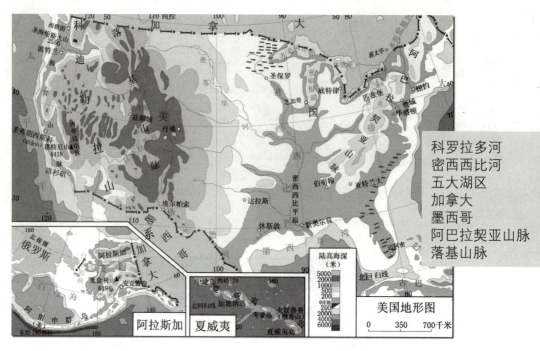

二、讨论 Discussion

中国土地沙漠化的影响及对策。
The influence and countermeasure on land desertification in China.

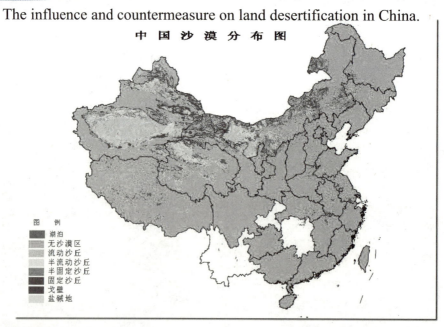

三、报告 Presentation

京杭大运河简介。
Introduction to the Great Canal of China.

English Version of the Text

The east and the southeast of China borders on the Pacific Ocean; the northern, northwestern and southwestern parts are desert and high mountains. The eastern part of China is the lower plain and hills, and the western is the ranges and plateaus. The east is low, and the west is high; If you look China on a map from the east to the west, you will find that it looks like some steps of a stair, and the view of each step is different. The highest peak in the world, the Qomolangma, is located in the western part of China; it is 8844.34 meters high.

There are many rivers in China. The Yellow River and the Changjiang River are two of the biggest rivers. The Heilongjiang River in the northeast, the Huaihe River in the middle, the Pearl River in the south, as well as the Lancangjiang River in the southwest are the very big rivers. The Great Canal from Beijing to Hanzhou is the longest and oldest man-made river in the world. There are many lakes in China too; for example, the Qinghai Lake and the Taihu Lake are vast and beautiful.

The eastern United States borders on the Atlantic Ocean and the western is connected to the Pacific Ocean. The south borders on the Gulf of Mexico. The north links to Canada and the southwest links to Mexico. The eastern, middle and southeastern parts of America are vast lowlands and plains; the western part is basin and grassland. The area of western coast is lowlands and plains, too. The east is low and the west is high in the United States also, but it looks like a big green carpet rather than stairs.

The Mississippi is located in the middle of America and flows into the Gulf of Mexico from the north to the south. The Colorado River and the Columbia River lie in the western part of America; they flow into the Pacific Ocean. The Five Great Lakes in the mid-north is the largest lake area in the world. The Appalachian Mountains in the east and the Rocky Mountains as well as the Sierra Nevada in the west affect the climate and geography of the United States very much.

第二课 城市
Chéngshì
Lesson 2　Cities

　　北京是中国的首都，她是中国的政治、经济和文化的中心。中南海(Zhōngnánhǎi)是中央政府的办公地点，在天安门广场的西北角。北京市、上海市、天津市和重庆市这四个城市由中央政府直接管理。上海是中国最大的城市，也是中国的金融中心。中国还有二十三个省、五个民族自治区和两个特别行政区。民族自治区和特别行政区在行政管理上相当于省。每个省的省会和自治区的首府，一般就是这个省或自治区最大的城市，也是政治、经济和文化的中心。香港和澳门分别是两个特别行政区。

　　除省会城市外，青岛、大连、苏州、洛阳(Luòyáng)、厦门(Xiàmén)、深圳(Shēnzhèn)等也都是中国很著名的城市。

美国的首都是华盛顿，白宫是联邦政府的办公地点，是美国的政治中心。但美国的经济和文化中心在纽约，华尔街 (Huá'ěr Jiē, the Wall Street) 和百老汇 (Bǎilǎohuì, Broadway) 都是全世界所关注的地方。美国共有五十个州，州基本相当于中国的省。与中国不同，一般来讲，州首府所在的城市并不是这个州最大的城市，也不是这个州的经济和文化中心。比如，华盛顿 (Huáshèngdùn, Washington) 州的首府是奥林匹亚 (Àolínpǐyà, Olympia) 市，但华盛顿州最大的城市却是西雅图 (Xīyǎtú, Seattle) 市；德克萨斯 (Dékèsàsī, Texas) 州的首府是奥斯汀 (Àosītīng, Austin) 市，但最大的城市却是休斯顿 (Xiūsīdùn, Houston) 市。纽约是世界上最大的城市之一，但她却不是纽约州的首府，纽约州的首府是奥尔巴尼 (Ào'ěrbāní, Albany) 市。

另外，旧金山、洛杉矶、芝加哥 (Zhījiāgē, Chicago)、费城 (Fèichéng, philadelphia)、亚特兰大 (Yàtèlándà, Atlanta)、底特律 (Dǐtèlǜ, Detroit)、迈阿密 (Mài'āmì, Miami) 等都是美国的大城市。

首都 shǒudū	capital		特别行政区 tèbié xíngzhèngqū	special administration region
政治 zhèngzhì	politics		相当于 xiāngdāngyú	correspond to
经济 jīngjì	economy		省会 shěnghuì	provincial capital
文化 wénhuà	culture		首府 shǒufǔ	provincial capital of autonomous region
政府 zhèngfǔ	government		一般 yìbān	commonly, currently
办公 bàngōng	work		分别 fēnbié	separate, different, part
地点 dìdiǎn	address, location		除……外 chú……wài	besides, except
广场 guǎngchǎng	square, plaza		著名 zhùmíng	famous, well known
直接 zhíjiē	direct		联邦 liánbāng	federation
管理 guǎnlǐ	management		关注 guānzhù	attention
金融 jīnróng	finance		州 zhōu	state
省 shěng	province		一般来讲 yìbān láijiǎng	generally speaking
民族自治区 mínzú zìzhìqū	national municipality, autonomous region			

专有名词 Proper Nouns

上海 Shànghǎi	a city of China		天津 Tiānjīn	a city of China

重庆 Chóngqìng	a city of China	白宫 Báigōng	the White House
青岛 Qīngdǎo	a city of China	纽约 Niǔyuē	New York
大连 Dàlián	a city of China	旧金山 Jiùjīnshān	San Francisco
苏州 Sūzhōu	a city of China	洛杉矶 Luòshānjī	Los Angeles
华盛顿 Huáshèngdùn	Washington		

课文理解 Understanding of the Text

一、判断 True-false questions

1. 北京是中国的首都，是政治、经济、文化中心。　　　□ 对　□ 错
2. 故宫是中国中央政府的办公地点。　　　　　　　　　□ 对　□ 错
3. 北京市、天津市、上海市和重庆市由中央政府直接管理。□ 对　□ 错
4. 中国的省会城市一般是这个省最大的城市。　　　　　□ 对　□ 错
5. 华盛顿市是华盛顿州的首府。　　　　　　　　　　　□ 对　□ 错

二、选择 Multiple choice

1. 中国有_____个直辖市？
   A. 3　　　　B. 4　　　　C. 5　　　　D. 6

2. 中国有_____个省和_____个民族自治区。
   A. 22　　　 B. 23　　　 C. 5　　　　D. 6

3. 下面的哪个城市是省会？
   A. 天津　　 B. 香港　　 C. 洛阳　　 D. 重庆　　 E. 没有

4. 华尔街是_____的一条街道。
   A. 北京　　 B. 上海　　 C. 天津　　 D. 纽约

5. 纽约州的首府是_____。
   A. 纽约　　 B. 奥尔巴尼市　　 C. 旧金山　　 D. 洛杉矶

三、问 答 Short answer questions

请在这张空白的中国地图上标出下列城市的位置：
Please mark the location of the following cities in the blank map of China below:

北京　上海　天津　重庆
香港　深圳　青岛　大连

信息链接
Information Link

http://city.cri.cn/
http://www.cncitymap.com/
http://www.cuew.com/
http://www.city-data.com/
http://www.suzhou.gov.cn/
http://www.chinatoday.com/city/a.htm
http://www.sfgov.org/

资料搜集
Data Collection

拉萨市 Lahsa

汉语拼音_____

乌鲁木齐市 Urumqi

汉语拼音_____

呼和浩特市 Huhehot

汉语拼音_____

银川市 Yinchuan

汉语拼音_____

南宁市 Nanning

汉语拼音_____

台北市 Taipei

汉语拼音_____

拓展活动 Extention

一、探索 Exploration

请填写下列表格：

Please complete the form below:

	苏州 Suzhou	旧金山 San Francisico
人口 Population		
面积 Area		
建城时间 Establishment time		

(续表)

所在省/州 Located in province/state		
2010年国内生产总值 GDP, 2010		
大学数量 Stat. of universities/colleges		
2010年学生人数 Stat. of students, 2010		
2010年失业率 Unemployment, 2010		
人均住房面积 Housing area per person		
主要产业 Main industry	1. 2. 3.	1. 2. 3.
文化特征 Cultural character	1. 2. 3.	1. 2. 3.
主要社会问题 Main social problems	1. 2. 3.	1. 2. 3.

二、讨论 Discussion

在中国，一个省的最大城市一般就是这个省的省会，而在美国，一个州的最大城市却往往不是这个州的首府，为什么？请从历史、文化、政治和经济的角度谈一下原因。

In China, why is the biggest city of a province the provincial capital generally, but in the United States, the state capital is not always the biggest city? Please explain the reason in the context of history, culture, politics and economy.

三、报告 Presentation

简述北京的历史。

Introduction to history of Beijing.

Beijing is the capital of China. She is the center of politics, economy and culture in China. The central government is located at Zhong Nan Hai, the northwest corner of Tian An Men Square. Four cities—Beijing, Shanghai, Tianjin and Chongqing are managed directly by the central government. Shanghai is the biggest city in China, and also is another economic center. There are 23 provinces, 5 national autonomous regions and 2 special administration regions in China. The national autonomous region and special administration corresponds to a province in administrative management. Generally speaking, the biggest city of a province or a national autonomous region is her capital, and her center of politics, economy and culture. Hong Kong and Macao are two special administration regions.

Besides the provincial capitals, Qingdao, Dalian, Suzhou, Luoyang, Xiamen and Shenzhen are some of the very well-known cities in China.

The capital of the United States is Washington, D.C.. The federal government is located in the White House. She is the center of politics of the country. However, the center of economy and culture of the United States is New York. Wall Street and Broadway are places that all of the world pays attention to. There are 50 states in the USA; each state corresponds to a province of China. Differently from China, the state capital is not her biggest city generally, and not the center of her economy and culture. For example, the capital of Washington State is Olympia, but the biggest city of the state is Seattle; Austin is the capital of Texas and Houston is her biggest city. New York is the biggest city in the world, but she is not the capital of New York state; her capital is Albany.

Furthermore, San Francisco, Los Angeles, Chicago, Philadelphia, Atlanta, Detroit, and Miami are some of the big cities in the United states.

第三课 王小明和汤姆·史密斯
Wáng Xiǎomíng hé Tāngmǔ · Shǐmìsī
Lesson 3 Wang Xiaoming and Tom Smith

中国是一个多民族的国家。汉族是主体民族，占人口总数的90.56%①。中国目前有五十六个民族，除汉族外，其他五十五个是少数民族。汉族主要居住在中国的东北部、东部、中部和南部。少数民族主要居住在北部、西北部和西南部。汉族和少数民族共同创造了"多元（各个民族的文化元素）一体（一个中国文化整体）"②的中国文化。

汉族 Han

藏族 Tibetan

维吾尔族 Vigur

中国各民族的姓名很有意思。汉族人姓在前，名在后，比如"王小明"。藏族人没有姓，只有名，如尼玛次仁(Nímǎcìrén, Nimaciren)。"尼玛"在藏语中是太阳的意思，"次仁"是长寿的意思。维吾尔族人名在前，姓在后，如伊力亚·库尔班(Yīlìyà Kù'ěrbān, Yiliya Kurban)，女孩子的名字里经常加上"古丽"(Gǔlì, Guli)，"古丽"在维吾尔语中是"花儿"的意思。

① 2005年人口普查数据。The data of the census of 2005.
② 参见《中华民族多元一体格局》，费孝通博士，中央民族大学出版社，2003年。
Ref. *the Structure of Unity of Chinese Pluralistic Society*, by Dr. Xiaotong Fei, published by The Central University For Nationalities Press, 2003.

美国是一个移民国家,是一个多族群的社会,仅仅在纽约,就可以听到一百七十多种语言。美国人口中欧洲后裔最多,他们名在前,姓在后,如汤姆·史密斯(Tāngmǔ Shǐmìsī, Tom Smith)。有人说,因为中国人特别注重家族观念,所以要把代表家族的姓放在名字前面,但这种观点不一定对。虽然大多数美国人的姓在名字的后面,但他们也很热爱自己的家庭。家族观念和姓的位置没有什么太大的关系,这只是语言习惯的问题。如果把"朱小飞"说成"小飞朱",听上去很像是"小肥猪",容易使人产生误解。

　　美国其他族群人的姓名也是多种多样的,很值得我们去讨论、研究。

词 汇 Vocabulary

主体 zhǔtǐ	main body	元素 yuánsù	factor
占 zhàn	account for, occupy	整体 zhěngtǐ	integration
目前 mùqián	at present, presently	长寿 chángshòu	longevity
少数 shǎoshù	minority	移民 yímín	immigrant
主要 zhǔyào	main, mostly	族群 zúqún	race, ethnic group
共同 gòngtóng	common, together	社会 shèhuì	society
创造 chuàngzào	create	仅仅 jǐnjǐn	only, just

后裔 hòuyì	descendant	位置 wèizhì	position, location
注重 zhùzhòng	pay importance to	关系 guānxi	relation, connection
家族 jiāzú	family	问题 wèntí	problem, question
观念 guānniàn	concept	误解 wùjiě	misunderstand
代表 dàibiǎo	represent	值得 zhíde	be worthy doing
观点 guāndiǎn	viewpoint		

专有名词 Proper Nouns

汉族 Hànzú	Han Nationality	维吾尔族 Wéiwú'ěrzú	Uigur
藏族 Zàngzú	Tibetan	欧洲 Ōuzhōu	Europe

课文理解 Understanding of the Text

一、判断 True-false questions

1. 中国只有汉族一个民族。 □对 □错
2. 中国有五十六个少数民族。 □对 □错
3. 中国的少数民族主要居住在北部、西北部和西南部。 □对 □错
4. 尼玛次仁是维吾尔族人的名字,伊力亚·库尔班是藏族人的名字。 □对 □错
5. 中国人和美国人都很重视家族观念。 □对 □错

二、选择 Multiple choice

1. 汉族主要居住在中国的东北部、_____部、_____部和南部，少数民族主要居住在中国的_____部、西北部和_____部。
   A. 西南部　　　B. 中部　　　C. 东部　　　D. 北部

2. 汉族人的名字是姓在_____，名在_____；而维吾尔族人的名字是姓在_____，名在_____。
   A. 前　　　　　B. 后

3. 总的来讲，中国文化是"多元一体"的文化。"多元一体"是什么意思？
   A. 中国文化主要是由汉族人创造的
   B. 中国文化主要是由少数民族创造的
   C. 中国文化是由汉族和少数民族共同创造的
   D. 中国文化是由外国人创造的

4. 中国有_____个少数民族。
   A. 53　　　　　B. 54　　　　　C. 55　　　　　D. 56

5. 美国人口中，_____人后裔最多。
   A. 亚洲　　　　B. 非洲　　　　C. 欧洲　　　　D. 北美洲

三、问答 Short answer questions

1. 照片里的中国人都穿上了传统的民族服装，请在照片下注明哪个是汉族，哪个是藏族，哪个是维吾尔族：
   These Chinese in the photos are wearing their traditional costumes. Please write who are Han people, Tibetan and Uigur under the photos:

　_____族　　　　　　_____族　　　　　　_____族

2. 请给自己取一个中文名字。
   Please give yourself a Chinese name.

信息链接 Information Link

http://www.chinesenames.org/
http://www.mandarintools.com/chinesename.html
http://www.tibetonline.net/
http://www.tibetculture.net/
http://www.chinaxinjiang.cn/
http://www.xjart.cn/
http://www.presscluboftibet.org/
http://www.tibetculturetour.com/
http://www.globosapiens.net/
http://www.chinaculture.org/
http://www.chinaculturecenter.org/

资料搜集 Data Collection

《百家姓》 A Collection of Chinese Surnames

汉语拼音_____

蒙古族 Mongolian

汉语拼音_____

藏族 Tibetan

汉语拼音_____

维吾尔族 Uigur

汉语拼音_____

回族 Hui Nationality

汉语拼音_____

壮族 Zhuang Nationality

汉语拼音_____

一、探索 Exploration

在空白中国地图上标注出藏族、维吾尔族、回族、蒙古族和壮族的主要居住地区。
Please mark the main living area of Tibetan, Uigur, Hui, Mongolian and Zhuang in the blank map of China below.

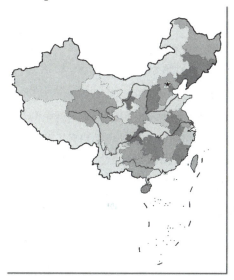

二、讨论 Discussion

课文里说"因为中国人特别注重家族观念,所以要把代表家族的姓放在名字前面,但这种观点不一定对",那么你对这个问题怎么看呢?
It is stated in the text that Chinese pay importance to the family conception, so they put their last names in the front of their first names; however, this viewpoint may not be right. What do you think of this?

三、报告 Presentation

调查一下你周围中国人的姓氏和民族,并做一个统计表展示出来。
Make a chart that shows different Chinese last names and nationalities around you.

English Version of the Text

China is a country with many nationalities. The main nationality is Han, accounting for 90.56% of the population. At present, there are 56 nationalities in China, other than Han; the others are minorities. Mostly, Han people reside in northeast, east, middle and south areas of China, and minorities reside in the north, northwest and southwest areas. Together, Han and minorities create Chinese culture in one integration (all of Chinese culture) with multiple factors (various cultural factors of each nationality).

The names of each nationality of China are very interesting. For Han people, their last names are in the front of their names, and first names in the rear, for instance, Wang, Xiaoming. Tibetans have no last name, but a first name, for instance, Nimaciren. In Tibetan, *nima* means the sun, and *ciren* means longevity. For the Uigur, their last names are in the rear of the names, and first names in the front, for instance, Yiliya Kurban. They often add the word, *Guli* to the names of girls; *guli* means flower in Uigur.

The United States is a immigration country, and a society with many races. In New York City alone, more than 170 languages can be heard. Most of the population is of European descent; their first names are in the front, and last names in the rear, for example, Tom Smith. Some people think that the Chinese pay homage to the family conception, so they put their last name in the front of their first names; however, this viewpoint may not be right. Although most of American last names are in the rear, Americans love their families very much. The family concept has nothing to do with the position of the last name; this is only a language convention. If Zhu Xiaofei is called as Xiaofei Zhu, it sounds like 小肥猪, a fat piggy, a misunderstanding could come out.

The use of names in other races in the United States is various, and it is worth discussing and researching.

第四课 故宫和白宫
Gùgōng hé Báigōng
Lesson 4 The Palace Museum and the White House

"故"字在汉语中是"老"和"旧"的意思。"故宫"就是"老宫殿",也叫"紫禁城",在北京市的中心,是中国明清两个朝代的皇宫。故宫于1406年开始建造,1420年基本完成,占地约723,600平方米(7,788,765.58平方英尺),共有8700多个房间。紫禁城作了五百年的皇宫,直到1911年,中国最后一个封建王朝——清朝结束。1925年,紫禁城改名为"故宫博物院",简称"故宫",并对外开放。[①]

故宫分成两个部分,前面的部分是皇帝的办公场所,后面的部分是皇帝的生活场所。故宫的建筑雄伟精美,是中国古代皇权的象征。

[①] 参考《中国大百科全书(第二版)》,中国大百科全书出版社,2009年。
Ref. *Encyclopedia of China*, Second Edition, published by Encyclopedia of China Publishing House, 2009.

"白宫"在汉语里就是"白色宫殿"的意思,在华盛顿特区,是美国总统的办公地点和官邸。白宫于1792年开始建造,1800年基本完成,占地73,000平方米(785,765平方英尺)。白宫的建筑地址是由美国第一任总统华盛顿选定的,但白宫的第一个主人却是第二任总统约翰·亚当斯(Yuēhàn Yàdāngsī, John Adams)。1800年白宫开始对外开放。

其实,白宫本来是红色的,它是1814年在英国军队烧毁后重建时染成白色的。和中国的故宫一样,白宫也是世界五大宫殿之一。它的设计者是詹姆斯·霍本(Zhānmǔsī Huòběn, James Hoban)。

词汇 Vocabulary

词	英文	词	英文
皇宫 huánggōng	royal palace	皇权 huángquán	imperial authority
基本 jīběn	basic, essence	象征 xiàngzhēng	indicate, symbol
平方 píngfāng	square	总统 zǒngtǒng	president
英尺 yīngchǐ	feet	官邸 guāndǐ	mansion
封建 fēngjiàn	feudalism	选定 xuǎndìng	select, make choice of
结束 jiéshù	end, finish	主人 zhǔrén	master
博物院(馆) bówùyuàn (guǎn)	museum	其实 qíshí	in fact, actually
对外 duìwài	foreign, external	军队 jūnduì	army, troop
开放 kāifàng	open	烧毁 shāohuǐ	burn
建筑 jiànzhù	build; building, construction	重建 chóngjiàn	rebuild
雄伟 xióngwěi	majesty, great	染 rǎn	dye
精美 jīngměi	fine	设计者 shèjìzhě	designer

专有名词 Proper Nouns

词	英文	词	英文
故宫 Gùgōng	the Palace Museum	明朝 Míngcháo	Ming Dynasty
紫禁城 Zǐjìnchéng	the Forbidden City	清朝 Qīngcháo	Qing Dynasty

课文理解
Understanding of the Text

一、判 断 True-false questions

1. 故宫又名紫禁城。　　　　　　　　　　　　　　　　□ 对　　□ 错
2. 故宫在上海。　　　　　　　　　　　　　　　　　　□ 对　　□ 错
3. 故宫作了八百年的皇宫。　　　　　　　　　　　　　□ 对　　□ 错
4. 1925 年，紫禁城改名为"故宫博物院"，简称
   "故宫"，并对外开放。　　　　　　　　　　　　　　□ 对　　□ 错
5. 白宫的设计者是林肯。　　　　　　　　　　　　　　□ 对　　□ 错

二、选 择 Multiple choice

1. 紫禁城又被称作_____。
   A. 老宫　　　　B. 旧宫　　　　C. 故宫

2. 中国的_____就是在紫禁城结束的。
   A. 元朝　　　　B. 明朝　　　　C. 清朝

3. 紫禁城现在是_____。
   A. 官邸　　　　B. 博物馆　　　C. 办公地点

4. 故宫分成两个部分，前面的部分是皇帝的_____场所，后面的部分是皇帝的_____场所。
   A. 锻炼　　　　B. 生活　　　　C. 购物　　　　D. 办公

5. 白宫本来是_____色的。
   A. 白　　　　　B. 红　　　　　C. 黄　　　　　D. 蓝

三、问 答 Short answer questions

查阅一下故宫的历史，编写一个简单的"故宫介绍"。
Look up the history of the Palace Museum and compile an introduction to it.

http://www.dpm.org.cn/
http://www.npm.gov.tw/
http://www.17u.com/
http://www.nj5161.cn/
http://www.chinahighlights.com/
http://www.chinamuseums.com/
http://www.whitehouse.gov/
http://www.2020site.org/

资料搜集 Data Collection

圆明园遗址 The Ruins of Yuanmingyuan

汉语拼音_____

天坛 The Heaven Temple

汉语拼音_____

颐和园 The Summer Palace

汉语拼音_____

太和殿 The Hall of Supreme Harmony

汉语拼音_____

拓展活动 Extention

一、探索 Exploration

以下是关于故宫的几张图片资料，请你谈谈它们反映出什么样的中国文化特点：

Below are some photos of the Palace Museum. Please discuss the Chinese cultural characteristics reflected in them:

二、讨论 Discussion

紫禁城在建成五百年后才对外开放,而白宫在建成的当年就对外开放了。请从历史、文化和政治的角度讨论一下其中的原因。

The Forbidden City was open to the public 500 years after its establishment, but the White House was open at the year of its establishment. Please discuss the reasons for this in the context of history, culture and politics.

三、报告 Presentation

除北京的故宫外,中国还有沈阳故宫、南京故宫和台北故宫,请演示一下这些故宫的历史,及与北京故宫的关系。

Besides the Palace Museum in Beijing, there are the Palace Museums in Shenyang, Nanjing and Taipei of China; please present the history of these Palace Museums, and their relationship with the Palace Museum in Beijing.

The Chinese character 故 means "old and past"; the Palace Museum is the old palaces, and is also called the Forbidden City. Located in the center of Beijing, this is the royal palace of the two Chinese dynasties of Ming and Qing. Begun to build in 1406, it completed almost in 1420; it is 723,600 sq. meters (7,788,765.58 sq. feet) and has over 8,700 rooms. The Forbidden City was the royal palace for 500 years until 1911, the year that the final dynasty of China, Qing ended. In 1925, it was renamed the Palace Museum, Gu Gong for short, and open to the public.

There are two parts in the Palace Museum: The front is the place where the emperor used to work, and the rear is a living space. The buildings are great and beautiful. The Palace Museum is the symbol of ancient Chinese imperial authority.

The White House means "the white palace" in Chinese. Located in Washington D.C., it is the office and mansion of the president of the United States. Begun to build in 1792, it almost completed in 1800; it is 73,000 sq. meters (785,765 sq. feet). The address of the White House was determined by the first president of the United States, George Washington, but her first master was the second president of the United States, John Adams. The White House was open to the public in 1800.

Actually, the White House was red; it was dyed white when being rebuilt after it was burned by the English army in 1814. Just as the Palace Museum of China, the White House is one of the top five palaces in the world. Her designer is James Hoban.

第五课 你好！
Lesson 5　Hello!

　　汉语是世界上使用人数最多的语言。汉语属于汉藏语系，共有七个大方言区。广东话，或称"粤（Yuè，Canton）语"，就是其中一种。每种方言在语音上区别较大，甚至不同方言区的人有时竟不能听懂对方说的话，因此需要用书写汉字的方式来交流。像"你好"这样两个简单的字，每种方言的说法也是不一样的。推广和学习汉语普通话的目的之一，就是要尽量消除方言间在语音上的差异，让大家能够又快又准地相互沟通。所以，学汉语最好就学普通话。普通话的语音是以北京话为标准的。

　　汉语有很长的历史，从古代汉语发展到现代汉语，在语音、词汇、语法和文字上都有很大的变化，广东话保留了一些古代汉语的语音特色。

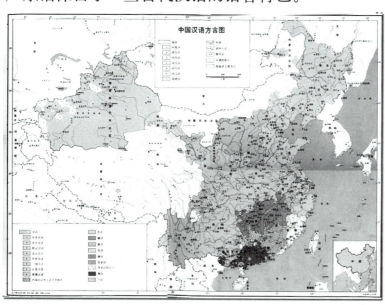

英语是美国的官方语言，也是美国使用人数最多的语言。美国英语是英语的一种方言。西班牙语(Xībānyáyǔ, Spanish)是美国的第二大语言。美国英语内部也存在一些方言，但与汉语不同，这些方言之间，人们是相互可以听懂的。

  世界上有很多人在使用或学习英语，使英语成了目前世界上的通用语。如果你说Hello，几乎人人都知道你在打招呼，尽管他根本就不会说英语。既然这样，那么，你现在为什么要学习汉语呢？对这个问题，每个汉语学习者的答案是不同的。你的答案又是什么呢？

词汇 Vocabulary

语系 yǔxì	phylum	沟通 gōutōng	communicate
方言 fāngyán	dialect	特色 tèsè	character, feature
语音 yǔyīn	pronunciation	官方 guānfāng	official
甚至 shènzhì	even	内部 nèibù	interior, inside
普通话 pǔtōnghuà	the standard Mandarin	存在 cúnzài	exist, be
消除 xiāochú	eliminate, avoid	通用 tōngyòng	general, current
差异 chāyì	different, diversity	几乎 jīhū	almost
准 zhǔn	precise, exact	打招呼 dǎ zhāohu	greet

根本 gēnběn	at all, fundamentality	答案 dá'àn	answer
既然 jìrán	even if		

专有名词 Proper Nouns

广东 Guǎngdōng	Canton	西班牙 Xībānyá	Spain

课文理解 Understanding of the Text

一、判断 True-false questions

1. 英语是世界上使用人数最多的语言。　　☐ 对　☐ 错
2. 汉语有七个大方言区。　　☐ 对　☐ 错
3. 汉语每种方言在语音上区别不大，人们能相互听懂。　　☐ 对　☐ 错
4. 普通话的语音是以北京话为标准的。　　☐ 对　☐ 错
5. 西班牙语是美国第二大语言。　　☐ 对　☐ 错

二、选择 Multiple choice

1. 汉语有_____个方言区。
   A. 5　　　　B. 6　　　　C. 7　　　　D. 8

2. 每种方言在语音上区别较大，甚至不同方言区的人有时竟不能听懂对方说的话，因此需要用_____的方式来交流。
   A. 翻译 (fānyì, interpret)　　B. 手语 (shǒuyǔ, sign language)　　C. 书写汉字

3. 推广和学习汉语普通话的目的之一，就是要尽量消除方言间的_____差异。
   A. 语法　　　B. 语音　　　C. 词汇　　　D. 文字

4. 汉语普通话的语音是以_____话为标准的。
   A. 广东   B. 上海   C. 北京   D. 天津
5. 美国英语的各个方言_____。
   A. 词汇不一样   B. 人们相互之间听得懂
   C. 拼写不一样   D. 语法不一样

三、问 答 Short answer questions

请看看中国每个方言区都包括了哪些省份，然后完成下面的表格：
Please look up what provinces are included in each dialect zone of China and complete the following chart:

方 言 Dialect	省 份 Provinces
北方话　North Dialect	
江浙话　Jiang-Zhe Dialect	
福建话　Fujian Dialect	
湖南话　Hunan Dialect	
江西话　Jiangxi Dialect	
客家话　Hakka	
广东话　Cantonese	

http://www.hhqq.net/
http://www.hanghua.net/
http://www.pthxx.com/
http://www.pinyinbao.com/

http://www.mandarintools.com/
http://www.ethnologue.com/
http://www.chinalanguage.com/dictionaries/index.php?module=home/
http://www.glossika.com/en/dict/

资料搜集
Data Collection

汉语拼音 Pinyin, Phonetic Transcriptions of Chinese Characters

汉语拼音_____

简化字 Simplified Chinese Character

汉语拼音_____

繁体字 Complicated Chinese Character

汉语拼音_____

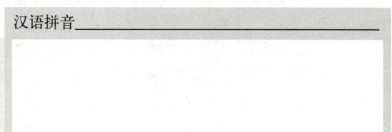

《新华字典》 The Dictionary of Xinhua

汉语拼音_____

一、探索 Exploration

请你身边的中国人说下列句子，听听他们在语音上的差别，并问问他们来自中国的哪个地方：

Ask Chinese people you know to speak the following sentences. Distinguish their pronunciation and ask them where they are from:

1. 你好！
2. 十四是十四，四十是四十。十四不是四十，四十不是十四。

二、讨论 Discussion

我们为什么要学习汉语？
Why do we learn Chinese?

三、报告 Presentation

中国的哪种方言最具影响力？
Which Chinese dialect is the most influential?

英语译文
English Version of the Text

Chinese is the most widely used language in the world. Chinese belongs to Han-Tibetan phylum and has seven main dialect zones. Guangdong Speech, or so-called Cantonese is one of them. Each dialect is different in pronunciation; even people in different dialect zones can not communicate with each other sometimes, so writing is needed. Ni Hao, hello in English—these two simple words are pronounced differently even in each dialect. One of the best ways to popularize and learn the standard Mandarin, Pu Tong Hua, is to try our best to avoid the dialect difference in pronunciation, and communicate fast and exactly. Therefore, if learning Chinese, it's better to learn the standard Mandarin, Pu Tong Hua. The pronunciation of Beijing speech is its standard.

Chinese has a long history; there are a great changes in pronunciation, vocabulary, grammar and character from the ancient Chinese and the modern Chinese, while Cantonese keeps some features in pronunciation from the ancient Chinese.

English is the official language of the United States and most of her people speak it. American English is a dialect of English. Spanish is the second popular language in the country. There are a few dialects in American English; unlike Chinese, they can be understood through speech alone.

Lots of people in the world are speaking or learning English; it makes English a widely-used language. If you say HELLO, it seems that people know you are greeting them though they may not be able to speak English. In this case, why learn Chinese now? Every Chinese learner has different answer to this question. What is yours?

第六课 厨房 Chúfáng
Lesson 6 Kitchen

中国菜是世界上最普及的菜肴之一。由于生活习惯不同，自然环境不同，中国菜分成八个主要的菜系：川（Chuān，四川省的简称）菜、粤菜、鲁（Lǔ，山东省的简称）菜、闽（Mǐn，福建省的简称）菜、苏（Sū，江苏省的简称）菜、浙（Zhè，浙江省的简称）菜、湘（Xiāng，湖南省的简称）菜和徽（Huī，安徽省的简称）菜。少数民族的菜肴则被称为"民族风味"，如新疆的"维吾尔族风味"、云南的"傣族风味"等。

中国汉族的餐饮文化充分表现出了农耕民族的饮食特点，食材丰富，烹饪手法多样。而蒙古族、藏族和维吾尔族的饮食文化又充分表现出了游牧民族的饮食特点，即以肉食为主，烹饪手法上以烤、煮为主。

汉族家常菜

蒙古族手把肉

藏族酥油

维吾尔族抓饭

美国白人族群的餐饮文化继承并发展了欧洲大陆的，发源于游牧类型和园艺类型的餐饮传统，与中国汉族的餐饮相比，食材较少，烹饪手法也比较

费城中国城里的一家中餐馆

单调。但从另一个角度讲，美国的餐饮文化又是特别发达的，因为，几乎世界上所有族群的饮食在这里都可以找到。

工业化食品是美国餐饮文化的一个显著特点，从主食到副食都可以买到已加工好的产品，它们只需回家加热，或稍稍处理一下就可以吃了。在美国，比萨店和汉堡快餐店、墨西哥餐厅随处可见，麦当劳 (Màidāngláo, McDonald's)、肯德基 (Kěndéjī, KFC) 和赛百味 (Sàibǎiwèi, Subway) 已经是世界知名的快餐品牌了。

普及 pǔjí	popular		手法 shǒufǎ	trick, technique
菜肴 càiyáo	dishes		游牧民族 yóumù mínzú	nomad
菜系 càixì	cuisine, school of		烤 kǎo	roast
风味 fēngwèi	flavor		煮 zhǔ	boil
充分 chōngfèn	fill, plenty		继承 jìchéng	inherit
农耕民族 nónggēng mínzú	cultivation people		发展 fāzhǎn	develop
食材 shícái	food material		发源 fāyuán	source, emanate (from)
烹饪 pēngrèn	cook		园艺 yuányì	gardening

类型 lèixíng	type	副食 fùshí	subsidiary foodstuff
传统 chuántǒng	tradition	加工 jiāgōng	process
单调 dāndiào	blankness, humdrum	随处可见 suí chù kě jiàn	can be found or seen everywhere
角度 jiǎodù	angle	品牌 pǐnpái	brand
主食 zhǔshí	main food		

专有名词 Proper Nouns

傣族 Dǎizú	Dai Nationality	蒙古族 Měnggǔzú	Mongolian

课文理解 Understanding of the Text

一、判断 True-false questions

1. 中国菜有六大菜系。　　　　　　　　　　　　　　□对 □错
2. "川"是四川省的简称，"鲁"是云南省的简称。　　□对 □错
3. "湘"是湖南省的简称，"闽"是福建省的简称。　　□对 □错
4. 新疆的"维吾尔族风味"、云南的"傣族风味"是少数民族菜肴。　　　　　　　　　　　　　　　　□对 □错
5. 工业化食品是美国餐饮文化的一个显著特点。　　□对 □错

二、选择 Multiple choice

1. 浙江的简称是_____，江苏的简称是_____。
   A. 京　　　　B. 苏　　　　C. 徽　　　　D. 浙

2. "傣族风味"是_____省的少数民族菜。
   A. 四川　　　　B. 贵州　　　　C. 云南　　　　D. 辽宁

3. _____饮食食材丰富，烹饪手法多样。
   A. 汉族　　　　B. 少数民族　　C. 工业化　　　D. 快餐

4. 汉族是_____，蒙古族是_____。
   A. 游牧民族　　B. 农耕民族

5. _____餐厅在美国最常见。
   A. 日本　　　　B. 越南　　　　C. 非洲　　　　D. 墨西哥

三、问 答 Short answer questions

请查阅一下中国城市的著名菜肴，并完成下列表格：

Please look up the famous dishes in Chinese cities and fill out the form:

城市 City	菜肴 Dishes		
北 京 Beijing	1.	2.	3.
上 海 Shanghai	1.	2.	3.
广 州 Guangzhou	1.	2.	3.
成 都 Chengdu	1.	2.	3.

信息链接 Information Link

http://www.ccicp.com/
http://www.zhms.cn/
http://chinesefood.about.com/
http://china.chinaa2z.com/china/

http://www.tastebook.com/
http://www.nicemeal.com/foodculture/
http://www.eatingchina.com/

资料搜集 Data Collection

北京烤鸭 Beijing Roast Duck

汉语拼音_____

麻婆豆腐 Mapo Tofu (stir-fried tofu in hot sauce)

汉语拼音_____

清真餐厅 Muslim Restaurant

汉语拼音_____

油 条 Fried Dough

汉语拼音_____

拓展活动 Extention

一、探索 Exploration

请按照下列菜谱选做一道中国菜：
Make a Chinese dish with the recipe below:

宫保鸡丁 Kung-Po Chicken

原料：

嫩鸡脯150克，花生米50克，干淀粉6克，花生油、葱段、辣油、白糖、酱油、湿淀粉、精盐、黄酒、干辣椒、香醋适量。

制做过程：

(1) 鸡脯肉除筋，开花刀，切成块状小丁，加鸡蛋白、干淀粉、精盐调拌均匀，放入旺猪油锅氽一下，将油沥干。

(2) 将干辣椒切成小丁，放入旺油锅（猪油也可，用花生油更好，可增加香味）煎，煎至呈金黄色，将鸡丁放入一起炒10秒钟。将葱段、黄酒、酱油、糖、醋、湿淀粉调和，倒入锅内炒拌数下，再将炒熟的花生入锅翻几下，最后加些辣油起锅即可。

要点：

炒时火要旺一些。

Materials:

150 grams tender chicken breast, 50 grams peanuts, 6 grams dry starch, peanut oil and some green onion pieces, spicy oil, sugar, soy bean oil, wet starch, fine salt, yellow wine, dry hot pepper and vinegar.

Operation:

(1) Take tendon apart from the chicken breast, cut it into small squares by oblique cut, put egg white, dry starch and fine salt on it and stir evenly. Poach the processed materials fast in a wok with hot peanut oil and then drop the lard out.

(2) Cut the hot pepper into small squares and fry it in hot oil (peanut oil is better to increase flavor) until it presents golden yellow. Add chicken breast squares and fry it with the hot pepper for 10 seconds. Stir green onion pieces, yellow wine, soy bean oil, sugar, vinegar and wet starch evenly and pour it into the wok and mix them, and then place the fried peanuts. Finally, add some spicy oil.

Notice:

The fire should be strong when frying.

维吾尔族羊肉抓饭 Uigur Polo

原料：

大米、羊排或羊肉骨头、胡萝卜、洋葱、花椒、料酒或白葡萄酒、姜、盐少许。

制做过程：

(1) 把羊排（或羊骨头）、胡萝卜洗净，胡萝卜擦丝，姜切片，洋葱切小块待用。

(2) 把水烧开，将羊排或羊骨头放在里面烫一下，捞出洗净，水倒掉。重新在锅里放水，水多些以便有较大量的汤。放入羊排（或羊骨头），加入料酒（或白葡萄酒）适量、姜片、花椒（数粒，不要太多），大火烧开，转小火炖。

(3) 淘米，晾略干。

(4) 待羊肉汤炖好，把姜片、花椒剔出，取出羊骨剔下肉切成一寸见方小块，若是羊排则直接切小块不剔骨。在电饭煲内加适量油，按下煮饭键，油开倒入洋葱和羊肉块翻炒一下，加入适量盐，再倒入胡萝卜丝，在上面直接倒上米，再把炖好的肉汤倒入，盖过米一寸左右。盖盖儿，煮。等煮饭键跳起来，用饭勺翻一下，若觉得不够熟再按煮饭键，至熟了跳起；或觉得不够烂，可再略加一点肉汤再煮一会儿。

Materials:

rice, mutton rib or mutton with bone, carrot, onion, pepper of Sichuan, cooking wine or white wine, ginger and salt.

Operation:

(1) Clean mutton rib or mutton with bone and carrot, rub carrot into floss, cut ginger into slices and cut onion into small pieces.

(2) Boil the water and burn the mutton rib or mutton with bone in it for a while, take them out and clean, then drop the used water. Pour water into the boiler again. There should be more water to have more soup. Put mutton rib or mutton with bone in, add cooking wine (or white wine), ginger slices, pepper of Sichuan (only grains, not too much), boil with strong fire and braise with mild fire.

(3) Clean the rice and dry it a little.

(4) When the mutton soup is ready, take out the ginger and pepper of Sichuan, pick the mutton away from the bone and cut into 1.3 inch squares. If the mutton ribs are used, cut them into small pieces without taking the bones out. Place some oil into the rice cooker, and press ON and fry onion and mutton when the oil is boiled. Add salt and carrot floss and place rice directly on it, then the cooked mutton soup. The soup must cover the rice around 1.3 inches over it. Cover the cooker and await until done. Turn the food over. Restart the cooker if the food is not cooked enough, or add some soup if the food is not soft enough.

二、讨论 Discussion

1. 中国菜反映了中国文化的什么特点？

What Chinese culture do the Chinese dishes indicate?

2. 中国菜和美国菜有什么区别？它们反映了什么不同的文化？
What's the difference between Chinese dishes and American dishes? And what different cultural characteristics do they indicate?

三、报告 Presentation

请演示饺子的来历及制作方法。
The origin and recipe of Chinese dumplings.

Chinese cuisine is one of the most popular dishes in the world. For the different of custom and environment, Chinese dishes can be divided into eight major schools of cooking, they are Sichuan Cuisine of Sichuan Province, Cantonese Cuisine of Canton Province, Lu Cuisine of Shandong Province, Min Cuisine of Fujian Province, Su Cuisine of Jiangsu Province, Zhe Cuisine of Zhejiang Province, Xiang Cuisine of Hunan Provine and Hui Cuisine of Anhui Province. The cuisine of the Minority peoples are called Minzu flavor, such as Uigur flavor of Xinjiang, Dai flavor of Yunnan, etc.

The cuisine culture of Chinese Han sufficiently represents the feature of cultivating people; the food material is rich, and the technique is of great variety. The cuisine culture of Mongolian, Tibetan and Uigur sufficiently represent the nomadic features. Their main food is meat; roasting and boiling are their main techniques.

The European descendants of the United States inherited and developed the cuisine culture from the types of nomadic and gardening people that come from Europe. Compared to Chinese cuisine, their food material is not rich, and their technique is simple. However, from a different angle, American cuisine culture is very developed, because the cuisine of almost all the races worldwide can be found here.

Industrialized food is another outstanding feature of American cuisine culture. Processed foods, which are subsidiary foodstuff made from main foods, can be purchased. They can be consumed after heating or processing easily. In the United States, fast food restaurants serving pizza and hamburger, and Mexican food restaurants can be found everywhere. McDonald's, KFC and Subway have been the famous fast food brands in the world.

第七课 城里和农村的住房
Chénglǐ hé nóngcūn de zhùfáng
Lesson 7 Houses in City and Countryside

  中国仍然是一个城乡差别比较大的国家,这一点在住房上就可以表现出来。在城里,居民基本上都是住在公寓里,叫单元房(unit)。单元房有居民租赁的,类似于美国英语中的 Apartment,也有居民购买的,类似于 Condo。随着收入的增加,又担心房子会越来越贵,现在越来越多的中国人在买房。

  在农村,农民的住房基本都是一家一个院落,类似于美国的 house。宅基地由国家分给农民使用,农民可按照自己的设计盖房。与城里的住房相比,有些农村的用水、用电等不是特别方便。

中国北方的一个普通农村

农民正在给新房上瓦

中国普通城市居民单元住房

　　美国的城乡差别不是很大，在城市学中，这个现象叫"城市郊区化(city suburbanization)"。除了市中心的公寓楼比较多外，居民的住房大都以院落住宅（house）为主，公寓为辅。难怪有些刚来美国的中国人说"美国看起来既像一个大农村，又像一个大城市"。

　　美国人的住宅一般都是从银行贷款买来的，所以，如果个人或国家的经济出现问题时，有些人还不起贷款，就不得不出售自己的房子。这种情况，在中国农村却很难看到。因为，宅基地是国家免费分给农民使用的，他们不用支付土地费，而建筑材料和人工又都很便宜。

第七课 城里和农村的住房
Lesson 7 Houses in City and Countryside

词汇 Vocabulary

仍然 réngrán	all the same, however, still	设计 shèjì	design
公寓 gōngyù	apartment	盖房 gài fáng	build a house
单元 dānyuán	unit	电 diàn	electricity
租赁 zūlìn	lease	方便 fāngbiàn	convenient
类似 lèisì	similar	……为主，……为辅 wéi zhǔ, wéi fǔ	as the main, ... as the subsidiary
购买 gòumǎi	buy, purchase	难怪 nánguài	no wonder, understandable
收入 shōurù	income	银行 yínháng	bank
增加 zēngjiā	increase	贷款 dài kuǎn	loan
担心 dānxīn	worry, care, be afraid	还 huán	return
院落 yuànluò	yard	出售 chūshòu	sell
宅基地 zháijīdì	housebase	支付 zhīfù	pay, payment
按照 ànzhào	according to	材料 cáiliào	material

课文理解 Understanding of the Text

一、判断 True-false questions

1. 和美国比，中国城乡差别不大。　　　　　　　　　　☐ 对　☐ 错

2. 中国的城市居民大都住在公寓里。 □ 对 □ 错
3. 随着收入的增加，又担心房子会越来越贵，现在越来越多的中国人在买房。 □ 对 □ 错
4. 中国农村的用水、用电比城市要方便。 □ 对 □ 错
5. 中国农民的宅基地是免费的。 □ 对 □ 错

二、选 择 Multiple choice

1. 在中国，农民 _____ 盖房。
   A. 必须按照政府的要求　　　B. 可以按照自己的设计
2. 在中国，与城里的住房相比，有些农村的用水、用电等 _____ 。
   A. 十分方便　　B. 更方便　　C. 不是十分方便　　D. 一样方便
3. _____ 美国人住在公寓里。
   A. 所有　　　B. 大部分　　　C. 一半　　　D. 有些
4. 刚来美国的中国人经常说，美国 _____ 。
   A. 既像大城市，又像大农村　　B. 是个大农村　　C. 不像大农村
5. 宅基地 _____ 免费的，（但）他们 _____ 支付土地费。
   A. 是　　　B. 不是　　　C. 不用　　　D. 要

三、问 答 Short answer questions

请调查下面中国四个城市最近三年中的平均住房价格，并填写表格：
Check the average property price of the latest three years of the four Chinese cities following and fulfill the form:

	_____年 Year of _____	_____年 Year of _____	_____年 Year of _____
北京 Beijiing			
上海 Shanghai			
广州 Guangzhou			
西安 Xi'an			

第七课 城里和农村的住房
Lesson 7 Houses in City and Countryside

信息链接
Information Link

http://www.121fang.com/
http://www.humsurfer.com/china-estate
http://www.homesandproperty.co.uk/
http://www.estateagencyinchina.com/
http://www.crei.cn/
http://www.zghouse.net/
http://www.beifan.com/067buildings/page01.html
http://www.greatbuildings.com/
http://www.chinatownconnection.com/
http://www.chinaacsc.com/Index.htm

资料搜集
Data Collection

商品房 Commodity Building

汉语拼音_____

廉租房 Low-rate Residential Building

汉语拼音_____

牧民定居 Herdsmen Settlement

汉语拼音_____

拓展活动 Extention

一、探索 Exploration

1. 下面三张照片是不同地区的中国传统农牧民住宅，请谈谈为什么会这样设计：

   Below are three pictures of the traditional residence of a Chinese peasant and herdsman. Please talk about their building design:

陕西省北部的窑洞
the cave house in the north of Shaanxi Province

江西省农村的吊脚楼
the wooden-legged building in the countryside of Jiangxi Province

草原蒙古包
Mongolian yurt on grassland

2. 中国沿海城市住房价格普遍高于西部城市价格的原因。
The reason why the property price of the coastal cities is higher than that of western cities in China.

二、报告 Presentation

从下列照片看文化因素对中国建筑设计和房屋布置的影响：
Comment on the influence of cultural factors on Chinese construction design and room layout in the following pictures:

国家图书馆
The National Library

中央电视台
CCTV(China Central Television)

客厅1
Living room 1

客厅2
Living room 2

In China, there is a great difference between urban and rural areas. This just can be seen by the residences. In towns, most of residents live in buildings, called unit buildings. The unit buildings for lease is called an apartment, similar to American English; the unit buildings for purchase are called condos, similar to American English. With increasing income and feeling anxious about rise in housing price, more and more people are purchasing their flats now.

In rural areas, the peasants' residences consist of one courtyard for one family, similar to houses in the United States. The peasant has free housebase provided to use by the government, and he can build a house by his design. Compared with residence in urban areas, the supplies of electricity and running water are not so convenient in some rural areas.

There does not exist a great difference between town and country in the United States; this is called city suburbanization in urbanology. Except more apartments around downtown areas, the most common residences are houses with a yard, and apartments are the subsidiary residences. No wonder some Chinese who have just come to the United States think and say that it looks like either a big countryside or a big city.

Most Americans borrow money from bank to buy a house. Once the economy of the individual or the country has trouble, some people cannot return their loan to the bank, and have to sell their property. This hardly happens in China rural areas, because the peasant's housebase is freely provided by the government, they are not required to pay land fees, and building material and manpower are rather cheap.

第八课　自行车和汽车
Zìxíngchē hé qìchē
Lesson 8　Bicycle and Automobile

　　中国被称为"自行车大国"。20世纪的60年代到80年代，自行车数量多的主要原因是因为人口多、收入低和汽车工业不发达，人们大都采用自行车作为交通工具。当然，从另一个角度讲，这也起到了健身和环保的作用。只要你留心观察，就可以发现那时的自行车基本都是生活用车款式，很少看到山地车和跑车等休闲、运动的款式。

　　从90年代到现在，随着经济的发展，公共汽车和私人汽车的数量在逐年增加。无论在城市还是乡村，有车的人越来越多。这同时带来了两个严重的问题——污染和交通堵塞。像北京这样的大城市就不得不针对私人汽车采取限制措施，并鼓励市民多采用公共交通工具和自行车出行。与其他国家一样，汽车交通问题一直困扰着城市管理者们。

美国是"汽车轮子上的国家"。这与美国国土面积大，而人口相对稀少有关系。除非你住在市中心，如果你没有一部汽车的话，上学、上班、购物、看病、拜访亲友等活动都会十分麻烦。与中国相比，美国的城市公共汽车不是很方便，线路和班次都比较少，用于长途交通的火车也不多，所以大多数人还是采用私人汽车出行。飞机是美国的主要远行工具。到了目的地机场后，租辆汽车继续前行，是很多人的选择。由于汽车产业太发达，每十个美国人中，大概就有一个人的工作与汽车相关。

　　骑自行车是美国人十分喜爱的一种运动休闲方式。我们经常能看到一部汽车的后面或顶上载着自行车在路上奔驰，这说明在美国自行车不是主要的交通工具，而只是一种运动休闲工具。

第八课 自行车和汽车
Lesson 8 Bicycle and Automobile

词汇 Vocabulary

世纪 shìjì	century	稀少 xīshǎo	rare, scarce
采用 cǎiyòng	use, adopt	除非 chúfēi	unless
交通 jiāotōng	transportation, communication	与……相比 yǔ……xiāngbǐ	comparing with
工具 gōngjù	tool	线路 xiànlù	route, line
健身 jiànshēn	do fitness, body building	班次 bāncì	frequency, tour (of bus or train)
环保 huánbǎo	environment protection	长途 chángtú	long distance
留心 liúxīn	pay attention to, take care of	辆 liàng	a measurement word for vehicles
观察 guānchá	observe	继续 jìxù	continue, keep on
休闲 xiūxián	leisure	奔驰 bēnchí	run
困扰 kùnrǎo	trouble, disturb, suffer	说明 shuōmíng	state, explain
相对 xiāngduì	corresponding, relative		

课文理解 Understanding of the Text

一、判断 True-false questions

1. 美国被称为"自行车大国"。　□ 对　□ 错
2. 过去中国自行车数量多的主要原因是因为人口多、收入低和汽车工业不发达。　□ 对　□ 错

3. 过去中国的自行车款式大都是运动休闲型的。　　　　□对 □错

4. 现在的中国，无论是城市还是乡村，有车的人越来越多。□对 □错

5. 太多的汽车带来了两个严重的问题：汽车涨价和上班太晚。

　　　　　　　　　　　　　　　　　　　　　　　　　□对 □错

二、选择 Multiple choice

1. 中国是一个自行车大国的意思是说 _____。
   A. 中国有很多自行车　　　　B. 中国的自行车很大

2. 中国 20 世纪 60 年代到 80 年代自行车很多的原因是 _____。
   A. 需要环保　　B. 汽车工业不发达　　C. 收入低

3. 骑自行车是美国人十分喜爱的一种 _____ 方式。
   A. 交通　　B. 社交　　C. 运动　　D. 教育

4. 从 20 世纪 _____ 年代以后，中国的汽车数量开始增加。
   A. 60　　B. 70　　C. 80　　D. 90

5. 越来越多的汽车给中国带来的严重问题是 _____。
   A. 人口减少　　B. 污染　　C. 交通方便　　D. 交通堵塞

三、问答 Short answer questions

1. 20 世纪 60 到 80 年代中国自行车数量巨大的原因是什么？
   Why did China have a large number of bicycles from the 1960s to the 1980s?

2. 汽车过多带来的问题是什么？
   What problems does it bring up that more and more people have their own automobiles?

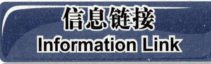

http://list.china.alibaba.com/buyer/offerlist/1204.html
http://www2.biketo.com/index.php
http://www.chinacars.com/

http://www.cacc.cc/
http://www.bikeforums.net/
http://bikeculturetheory.wordpress.com/
http://www.chinesebikes.net/
http://www.chinariders.net/
http://www.naturalnews.com/pollution.html
http://www.ep.net.cn/
http://www.chinaenvironment.com/
http://www.fastcompany.com/tag/american-auto-culture

资料搜集
Data Collection

动车组 Bullet Train

汉语拼音_____

青藏铁路 Qinghai-Tibet Railroad

汉语拼音_____

川藏公路 Sichuan-Tibet Highway

汉语拼音_____

塔里木沙漠公路 Tarim Desert Highway

汉语拼音_____

拓展活动
Extention

一、探索 Exploration

观察下面的图片，谈谈中国文化对汽车装饰的影响：
Please observe the following photos carefully, and talk about how the culture influences the auto decoration:

二、讨论 Discussion

在中国和美国推广电动自行车好不好？

Would it be good to promote the electric power bike in China? What about in the United States?

三、报告 Presentation

比较一下汽车对中国和美国城市文化的影响。

The comparison between the auto influence in the urban culture of China and the United States.

China is called "Kingdom of bicycles". From the 1960s to the 1980s, the main reasons why China had a large number of bicycles are due to her huge population, the low income and the developing auto-industry. People generally use bicycles as the reliable transportation. From another point of view, of course, this contributes to good health and environmental protection. If one observed carefully, one could find that the bicycles at the time were of daily life style, and mountain bikes and the racing bikes were hardly found.

From the late 1990s to the present, along with economic development, the amount of buses and private automobiles has increased gradually year by year. Whether in the town or countryside, more and more people have their own automobiles. This brings about two serious problems, pollution and traffic jams. The big cities, such as Beijing, have to make more rules to control the private automobiles, and encourage the residents to use buses and bicycles more. Just like other countries, the city administrations are suffering from the auto-transportation problem.

The Unites States is a "Country on auto-tires". This relates to her vast land and comparatively smaller population. Unless you live downtown, if you don't have a car, there will be a lot of trouble to go to school, to work, to the store, to see the doctor and to visit friends and relatives. Compared with China, the urban buses in the Unites States are not very convenient to take; the routes and frequency are limited. There are not so many trains for long distance transportation too. That is why most of the people drive their car to travel. The airplane is the main means for long distance traveling. When arriving at the airport, to rent a car to move on is common choice for many people. Due to the over-developed auto-industry, one in ten Americans must have a job in the auto-related industry.

Cycling is one of favorite sport leisures in America. In the United States, one often sees a running car with a bicycle on its top or attached to its trunk. This shows the bicycle is not a main transportation mean, but only a tool for leisure and sport.

第九课 工资单与税
Lesson 9　Payroll and Tax

在许多人的观念中，除了学生和失业的人之外，只要是有工作的人，就应该有工资单。但在中国，八亿农民虽有收入，但他们却没有工资单。他们不为雇主工作，土地使用权和大部分农业机械的所有权是农民自己的，在土地上种植什么也由自己来决定，出售农产品的利润所得也由自己来支配。2006年，在中国持续征收了2600多年的农业税被政府正式取消，这大大减轻了农民的经济负担。

农民庆祝取消农业税

在中国，有工资单的人在数量上远远少于没有工资单的农民，他们一般都是政府公务员、教师、

上海一个汽车工人的工资单

医生、艺术工作者、公司职员、工人和从事服务行业的人士等。当一个人的收入达到一定程度时,就要向国家缴纳个人所得税。农民如果到企业上班,虽然身份还是农民,但就会有工资单了。

在美国,只要你工作,你就一定会有工资单,因为你有给国家缴税的义务,工资单是你缴税的一个重要依据。从个人所得税的税率上来看,美国的税率远远高于中国,政府利用这些庞大税金构建了社会福利制度,使人们在失业、上学、就医等方面有了社会保障。

另一个与中国的明显差别是,在美国,同一单位里的职员个人收入的差距是比较大的。在中国传统文化中,"相对平均,注重稳定"是一个重要内容。这种思想反映在工资收入上,就是职务差别和个人对公司的贡献差别不能只是用工资多少来表示。而美国是一个主张竞争的社会,单位里人员流动很频繁。因此,职位较高、贡献较大、工作年限较长的人的工资就往往会高出很多。随着中国市场经济的发展,中国企业中工资的奖励因素也越来越高了。

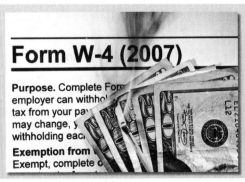

第九课 工资单与税
Lesson 9 Payroll and Tax

词汇
Vocabulary

雇主 gùzhǔ	employer
农业 nóngyè	agriculture
机械 jīxiè	machine
所有权 suǒyǒuquán	ownership
利润 lìrùn	profit
支配 zhīpèi	dominate
持续 chíxù	continue
征收 zhēngshōu	collect
减轻 jiǎnqīng	abate, reduce
负担 fùdān	burden, weight
职员 zhíyuán	staff
从事 cóngshì	deal with, work in
服务行业 fúwù hángyè	service industry
缴纳 jiǎonà	pay
个人所得税 gèrén suǒdéshuì	personal income tax

缴税 jiǎo shuì	pay tax
义务 yìwù	obligation
依据 yījù	proof
社会福利 shèhuì fúlì	social welfare
保障 bǎozhàng	guarantee, ensure
明显 míngxiǎn	obvious
差距 chājù	difference, gap
平均 píngjūn	average, even
稳定 wěndìng	stabilization
职务 zhíwù	post, duty
贡献 gòngxiàn	contribute, offer up
竞争 jìngzhēng	competition
频繁 pínfán	frequent
奖励 jiǎnglì	prize

课文理解
Understanding of the Text

一、判断 True-false questions

1. 中国的农民没有收入。　　　　　　　　　　　　　□ 对　□ 错
2. 中国的农民不为雇主工作。　　　　　　　　　　　□ 对　□ 错
3. 土地使用权和大部分农业机械的所有权是农民自己的。□ 对　□ 错
4. 2006年中国政府开始向农民征收农业税。　　　　　□ 对　□ 错
5. 美国政府利用庞大的税金构建了社会福利制度。　　□ 对　□ 错

二、选择 Multiple choice

1. 中国农民虽有收入，（但）他们_____工资单。
   A. 也有　　　B. 拒绝　　　C. 没有　　　D. 接受
2. 在中国，土地的_____是农民自己的，大部分农业机械的_____也是农民自己的。
   A. 使用权　　B. 所有权　　C. 处罚权　　D. 没收权
3. 中国农民出售农产品的利润由_____支配。
   A. 政府　　　B. 雇主　　　C. 农民自己　D. 工人
4. 2006年，在中国持续征收了2600多年的_____被政府正式取消。
   A. 个人所得税　B. 农业税　　C. 消费税　　D. 购置税
5. 在美国，纳税的一个重要依据是_____。
   A. 购物单　　B. 菜单　　　C. 工资单　　D. 保险单

三、问答 Short answer questions

请查阅1949年至2009年60年间，中国土地制度的变化，并完成下表：
Look up the changes of land policies of China during the 60 years from 1949 to 2009 and fill in the form below:

	时间 Time	基本内容 Basic Information
土地改革时期 Land Reformation Period		
合作社时期 Cooperativization Period		
人民公社时期 People's Commune Period		
家庭联产承包责任制时期 Household Contract Responsibility Period		

信息链接
Information Link

http://www.1shai.com/

http://www.bigongzi.com/default.aspx?step=1

http://www.taxinfo123.com/

http://pindao.nongmintv.com/

http://www.salary.com/

http://www.payscale.com/

http://www.abroadchina.org/salary.asp

http://cn.countrysearch.tradekey.com/salary-calculator.htm

http://www.worldwide-tax.com/china/indexchina.asp

http://www.capitaltaxconsulting.com/international-tax/china/chinese-income-tax/

http://www.farmer.gov.cn/

资料搜集 Data Collection

车辆购置税 Vehicle Acquisition Tax

汉语拼音_____

车船使用税 The Tax of Vehicles and Vessels

汉语拼音_____

房产税 House Tax

汉语拼音_____

《中华人民共和国个人所得税法》 *The Law of the People's Republic of China on Individual Income Tax*

汉语拼音_____

一、探索 Exploration

现在在中国的互联网上流行"晒工资",就是把自己的工资单公开出来给大家看。请问这是为什么?美国会不会出现"晒工资"的现象?请口头或书面回答这些问题。

To insolate one's salary on the internet is popular in China presently; it means to disclose one's payroll to the public. Why does it happen? Is it possible for Americans to do it? Please answer these questions in speech or writing.

参考:

(1) 中国工资结构一般包括以下内容:基础工资、岗位补贴、效绩工资、加班补贴、洗理补贴、电费补贴、交通补贴、独生子女补贴、医疗保险、养老保险、住房公积金等。

(2) 某网站统计的工资行业排行榜

  第一:电力、电信等国有企业,全国平均收入在 3000 元 / 月以上;

  第二:国税、地税、工商、海关、银行、财政等部门,全国平均收入
    在 2000 元 / 月以上;

  第三:政府职能部门,全国平均收入在 1000 元 / 月以上。

(3) 中国国民收入中,工资只占其中一部分,另外还有奖金和其他收入。

比如教师，除工资外，还有课时费及奖金等。有的行业中，工资甚至是收入的一小部分。

Ref.

(1) The items of Chinese payroll generally include basic salary, post allowance, performance salary, overtime allowance, bath & haircut allowance electricity allowance, transportation allowance, singleton allowance, medicare, endowment insurance, residence accumulation fund, etc.

(2) Industry rank of salary counted by a website:

1st, the state-owned industries of electric power, communication, RMB3000/mo, average countrywide;

2nd, the government departments of state tax, local tax, industry management, custom, bank, finance, RMB 2000/mo, average countrywide;

3rd, the government functional departments, RMB 1000/mo, average countrywide.

(3) The salary is only a part of the national income of China, besides prize and other income. For example, teacher's income includes class hour allowance and prize and so on besides the salary. Regarding some industries, salary is only a little part of the income.

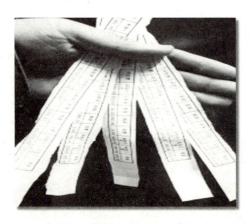 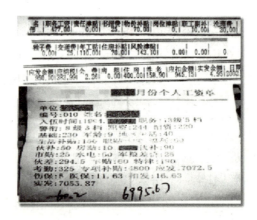

二、讨论 Discussion

中国为什么要取消农业税？

Why was the agricultural tax abolished in China?

三、报告 Presentation

中国和美国低收入人群形成原因。
The reason why low income people come into being.

In many people's opinion, except students and the jobless, if a person is employed, he must have a payroll. However, eighty million Chinese peasants have income, but they don't have a payroll. They don't work for any employers, the land access and the ownership of most of the agricultural machines are of their own, they determine what to plant in the soil, and dominate the profit from selling their agricultural products. In 2006, the agriculture tax that had been collected for 2,600 years continuously in China was abolished by the government. This lightened the peasants' economic burden greatly.

People who have a payroll are much fewer than people who are peasants in China. Generally, they are government officials, teachers, doctors, artists, company staff members, workers and persons who work in the service industry. When a person's income reaches a certain level, he will have to pay personal income tax to the country. If a peasant works in an enterprise, will he have a payroll, although his identity is still a peasant.

In the United States, only if you have a job, must you have a payroll, because you are obliged to pay tax to the government, and payroll is a very important proof for paying tax. The rate of personal income tax in the United States is much higher than that of China. The government makes use of the giant tax to set up a comparatively excellent system of social welfare. It offers people the good social guarantee for unemployment, going to school, hospitalization, etc.

Another obvious difference from China is, in the United States, there is a wide income gap among staff members in the same enterprise. In Chinese traditional culture, being relatively average and acquiring stability is very important. The idea behind salary is the difference of post, and individual contribution can not be represented by the salary only. The United States is a society of competition; people often change their jobs among enterprises. Therefore, people who are in higher postions, who make bigger contributions, and work for a longer time, have a much higher salary than others. Along with the development of a market economy in China, the prize factor in salary will become higher and higher in Chinese enterprises.

第十课　挂号 (Guà hào)

Lesson 10 Registration for Hospital Treatment

　　在中国看病，要在诊断前挂号。如果需要普通医生看病的话，挂号并不难。如果要找专家看病，这种号叫"专家号"。要是挂"专家号"就困难一些了，甚至还会出现通宵排队挂号和"医院黄牛党"的现象。

　　由于中国的公费医疗制度正在逐步转化为社会医疗保险制度，农民的医疗问题也在逐步解决，在这个过程中，难免出现一些不正常的情况。比如，一个普通的感冒，明明小医院就可以治好，但有人偏要去大医院挂号看病。现在，随着社区医院和医疗制度的改革，这种情况已有所好转。现在有些医院采取的互联网挂号，有效地制止了"黄牛党"的不良行为。

由于人口数量、医疗保险和社会福利制度的差异，在美国看病和在中国看病完全不同。如果病情不属于急诊，病人需要提前给自己的家庭医生打电话，预约看病时间。如果是急诊，就要去医院挂号，等医生诊断。

如果病人认为需要找技术更高的专家看病，可以通过互联网查到专家的专业特长和联系办法，告诉专家病情如何。如果专家同意为病人诊断，他就会为病人安排好看病的时间。所以，中国的专家号和美国的"专家号"也是不同的。

诊断 zhěnduàn	diagnose	公费 gōngfèi	at public expense
专家 zhuānjiā	specialist	医疗 yīliáo	medical care
通宵 tōngxiāo	all night	保险 bǎoxiǎn	insurance
黄牛党 huángniúdǎng	scalper	逐步 zhúbù	gradually

解决 jiějué	solve, settle	互联网 hùliánwǎng	internet
过程 guòchéng	process	制止 zhìzhǐ	stop, hold out
难免 nánmiǎn	unavoidable	病情 bìngqíng	disease, patient's condition
治好 zhìhǎo	recovery, heal	属于 shǔyú	belong to
偏 piān	insist on	急诊 jízhěn	emergency
社区 shèqū	community	预约 yùyuē	reserve
改革 gǎigé	reform	通过 tōngguò	through, by, pass
好转 hǎozhuǎn	get better		

课文理解 Understanding of the Text

一、判断 True-false questions

1. 在中国看病,不需要在诊断前挂号。　　　　　　　　　　□ 对　□ 错
2. 挂"专家号"比较容易一些。　　　　　　　　　　　　　　□ 对　□ 错
3. 由于挂"专家号"比较难,就出现了通宵排队挂号和
"医院黄牛党"的现象。　　　　　　　　　　　　　　　　□ 对　□ 错
4. 中国的公费医疗制度正在逐步转化为社会医疗保险制度。□ 对　□ 错
5. 美国的医院和中国一样,也有"黄牛党"。　　　　　　　□ 对　□ 错

二、选择 Multiple choice

1. 如果要找专家看病,这种号叫"_____"。
   A. 医生号　　B. 黄牛号　　C. 专家号

2. 在中国,要请普通医生看病,挂号比较_____,要是请专家看病,挂

号就_____了。
   A. 难   B. 容易

3. 中国正在从_____。
   A. 公有制逐步转变为私有制
   B. 公费医疗制度逐步转变为社会医疗保险制度
   C. 社会医疗保险制度逐步转变为公费医疗制度

4. 现在中国有些医院采取_____挂号，制止了黄牛党的不良行为。
   A. 排队   B. 电话   C. 互联网

5. 在美国看急诊，应该怎么做？
   A. 给医生打电话   B. 去医院挂号   C. 通过互联网查找专家

三、问 答 Short answer questions

查阅北京协和医院的历史，并写出简介。
Look up the history of Beijing Union Medical College Hospital and compile an introduction to it.

信息链接
Information Link

http://yyk.39.net/
http://www.pharmnet.com.cn/tcm
http://www.cnzy.com.cn/

http://www.zyzyyd.com/jjekeezr/wlxx/yd/fff.htm
http://www.cintcm.com/opencms/opencms/index.html
http://www.mib.org.cn/
http://www.mca.gov.cn/
http://www.moh.gov.cn
http://www.chinesemedicinesampler.com/
http://www.chinesemedicinenotes.com/
http://www.tibetanmedicine.com/
http://www.mongolia-web.com/
http://www.china.org.cn/

赤脚医生 Barefoot Doctor

汉语拼音_____

中医 Chinese Traditional Doctor

汉语拼音_____

藏医 Tibetan Traditional Doctor

汉语拼音_____

蒙医 Mongolian Traditional Doctor

汉语拼音_____

维吾尔医 Uigur Traditional Doctor

汉语拼音_____

一、探索 Exploration

访问一家你所在城市的中医诊所。访问前要写好调查提纲。
Visit a Chinese traditional medicine clinic located in your city. Prepare a questionaire syllabus before your visit.

二、讨论 Discussion

中医科学吗?
Is Chinese traditional medicine scientific?

三、报告 Presentation

文化对医学的影响。
How a culture impacts medicine.

A treatment registration is required if you have to see a doctor in China. If you need a general doctor to treat you, it is not hard to register. If you need a specialist to treat you, the registration becomes so-called specialist reservation, Zhuan Jia Hao. To make a specialist reservation is somewhat difficult. You even need to stand in a line to register all night, and hospital ticket scalpers appear.

The Free medicare system is transforming to the Social Medicare system in China.

The problems of medicare for peasants are being solved gradually. During the period, it is unavoidable to produce some deviations. For example, someone prefers going to a big hospital for treatment rather than a small hospital for just a common cold. At present, along with the reformation of the community hospital and medical system, this has been getting better. Some hospitals have internet application for registration nowadays, which effectively stopped scalpers.

Because of the population, medicare and social welfare system, it is quite different to see doctor in the United States from that in China. If not in an emergency, the patient needs to make a call to his family doctor in advance for reservation. If in an emergency, the patient needs to make a treatment registration in the hospital to see the doctor.

If a patient thinks that he needs to see a specialist with better techniques, he can look up the qualifications and contact of the specialist on the internet, and state his disease. If the specialist agrees to diagnose, he will make an appointment with the patient. So the Zhuan Jia Hao, specialist reservation in China is different from the one in the United States.

第十一课 餐厅里的热闹与安静
Lesson 11　The Noise and the Quietness in Restaurants

有人说，中国人看起来性格含蓄内向，但他们在餐厅里吃饭的时候，为什么那么热闹呢？其实，你只要仔细观察，并了解一下中国文化，答案自然就有了。如果是一家人在餐厅吃饭，往往是很安静的，但亲戚朋友在一起聚会，人多话多，声音自然就高了一些。中餐的品种大概是世界上最丰富的。中国人喜欢多安排些菜品招待客人，菜少，或者菜不够，主人就会觉得没面子，没照顾好客人。面对一桌子丰盛的菜肴，如果是你，可能也要忍不住大声说几句呢。

中国人宴请宾客，必须要有酒，这就是中国人说的"无酒不成席"。传统中国酒的度数都相当高，因为酒精的刺激，说话的音量也就比平常高了。在中国，酒甚至是饭的代名词。别看招牌上写的是"酒馆"，其实是"饭馆"。餐厅表现出了中国人的娱乐精神。

与中国人相比，美国人在餐厅里就安静了很多。其原因既有文化因素，也跟西餐的特点有关。美国人，特别是欧洲移民，继承了欧洲传统的饮食习惯，喜欢在就餐时，边吃边小声交谈，这样既保护了个人隐私，又不影响邻桌。另外，与中餐"共餐制"不同的"分餐制"、较为复杂的就餐程序和使用起来比较复杂的餐具，也许都会使人更安静一些，以免破坏了餐桌上的和谐气氛。

值得一提的是，吃西餐时一般也喝酒，但不像中国人那样把酒看得很重要。酒是配合饭菜的，当然，也为大家助兴，但真正喝酒的地方是酒吧。在中国的传统文化中，是没有相当于西方文化中的酒吧的地方的。所以你可以把中国人在餐厅的热闹，想象成在酒吧里的感觉。

第十一课 餐厅里的热闹与安静
Lesson 11 The Noise and the Quietness in Restaurants

词汇 Vocabulary

热闹 rènao	lively, liveliness		娱乐 yúlè	entertainment
性格 xìnggé	character		精神 jīngshén	spirit
含蓄 hánxù	connotation, implicative		隐私 yǐnsī	privacy
内向 nèixiàng	diffidence, introverted		共餐制 gòngcānzhì	Chinese serving
亲戚 qīnqi	relation, relatives		分餐制 fēncānzhì	individual serving
招待 zhāodài	entertain, receive (guests)		复杂 fùzá	complex
照顾 zhàogù	take care of		程序 chéngxù	program, procedure
丰盛 fēngshèng	rich		和谐 héxié	harmonious, peaceful
宴请 yànqǐng	entertain		气氛 qìfēn	mood, atmosphere
无酒不成席 wú jiǔ bù chéng xí	this is not a real banquet if no liquor is served		配合 pèihé	cooperate
刺激 cìjī	activate, stimulate		助兴 zhùxìng	liven things up, add to the fun
音量 yīnliàng	volume		想象 xiǎngxiàng	imagine, dream
招牌 zhāopái	signboard			

课文理解
Understanding of the Text

一、判断 True-false questions

1. 中国人的性格比较含蓄、内向。　　　　　　　　　　□ 对　□ 错
2. 中国人在亲戚朋友聚会时，都要保持安静。　　　　　□ 对　□ 错
3. 中国人喜欢多安排些菜品招待客人，认为这样做有面子。□ 对　□ 错
4. 一般来讲，中国人宴请宾客是要准备酒的。　　　　　□ 对　□ 错
5. 中国的酒馆就是西方的酒吧。　　　　　　　　　　　□ 对　□ 错

二、选择 Multiple choice

1. 如果菜少了，中国主人有时会觉得_____。
   A. 没手　　　B. 没脚　　　C. 没头　　　D. 没面子
2. 由于_____的刺激作用，人们说话的声音也就大了。
   A. 主食　　　B. 菜　　　　C. 酒精　　　D. 餐具
3. 在_____里，酒馆和饭馆是同义词。
   A. 英文　　　B. 法文　　　C. 中文　　　D. 德文
4. 美国人在吃饭时小声交谈，是为了保护个人_____。
   A. 财产　　　B. 隐私　　　C. 文件　　　D. 爱好
5. 你可以把中国人在餐厅的热闹，想象成在_____里的感觉。
   A. 商场　　　B. 机场　　　C. 酒吧　　　D. 体育馆

三、问答 Short answer questions

1. 为什么中国人在餐厅聚会时会比较热闹？
   Why are the Chinese people so lively when they have dinner in a restaurant?
2. 酒吧和酒馆有什么区别？
   What is the difference between a bar and a restaurant?

第十一课 餐厅里的热闹与安静
Lesson 11 The Noise and the Quietness in Restaurants

http://www.cnyiyin.com/
http://www.ccas.com.cn/
http://www.wenyi.com/
http://www.jiuwenhua.org/
http://www.cnjwh.com/
http://www.chinesefolklore.com/
http://www.nicemeal.com/foodculture/
http://www.travelchinaguide.com/intro/cuisine.htm
http://www.chinatravel.com/facts/chinese-food/
http://www.shanghaifinance.com/food/chinesewine.php
http://www1.american.edu/ted/baiju.htm
http://www.searchforvideo.com/society-and-culture/drinks/baijiu/
http://www.chinese-forums.com/
http://soulfoodonline.net/
http://www.soulfoodandsoutherncooking.com/

资料搜集 Data Collection

全聚德烤鸭 QJD Roast Duck

汉语拼音_____

满汉全席 Royal Feast of the Complete Manchu-Han Courses

汉语拼音_____

茅台酒 Mao-tai Chiew

汉语拼音_____

划拳 Drinking Game

汉语拼音_____

拓展活动
Extention

一、探索 Exploration

现在中国的酒吧也很多，比如，在北京就有两条很有名的酒吧街。一条是靠近使馆区的三里屯酒吧街，一条是靠近北海公园的后海酒吧街。通过照片，请你谈谈它们的异同。

Nowadays, there are lots of bars in China. For example, there are two well-known bar streets in Beijing. One is San Li Tun bar street near the embassy zone; the other is Hou Hai bar street near Beihai Park. Looking at the pictures, please discuss their differences.

三里屯的酒吧
Bars in San Li Tun

后海的酒吧
Bars in Hou Hai

二、讨论 Discussion

如何在中国参加宴会？
How to join a Chinese banquet?

三、报告 Presentation

酒对中国文化的影响。报告应介绍酒的起源、酿造、器具、礼俗、品牌和人物等。
Liquor's influence on Chinese culture, including origin, brewage, ware, custom, brand and famous industry-related people.

It is said that Chinese people look reserved and diffident, but why are they so lively when they have dinner in a restaurant? Actually, only if you observe carefully and understand some Chinese culture, you will know the answer easily. When a family has dinner in a restaurant, they are usually very quiet. Nevertheless, when your relatives or friends have a party, the more people there, the more words, and the voices will be raised naturally. The variety of Chinese dishes is probably the richest in the world. A Chinese person would likely serve more dishes than his guests can eat, to honor them. Just enough dishes to adequately feed his guests will make the master lose face, and his guests will think he doesn't treat them well. Facing a table of rich dishes, maybe you also cannot help speaking out loud.

Liquor must be served when a Chinese treats his guests. The Chinese think that it is not a real banquet if no liquor is served. The alcohol content of traditional Chinese liquor is higher. Speaking voice will be louder than usual for those under alcoholic stimulation. In China, a sign for a pub means restaurant because "alcohol" means the same thing as "food". Therefore, restaurants reflect the spirit of Chinese entertainment.

Compared with the Chinese, Americans in restaurants sound quiet. The reasons relate to cultural factors and the character of western dishes. Americans, especially the immigrants from Europe, inherited a European table manner, speaking in a low voice while eating. This not only protects privacy, but also doesn't bother the nearby table. In addition, the individual serving is different from Chinese serving; the comparatively complex repasting process, and various dishware may make people quieter to avoid breaking the harmonious atmosphere at the table.

The point which is worth mentioning is that liquor is served in western cuisine, but it is not as important as it in China. Wine is served with food, and surely, it livens people up. The bar is the place for serving liquor. In Chinese traditional culture, there is not anything similar to the bar in the western culture. Therefore, you can imagine the noise in a Chinese restaurant is like the feeling of being in a bar.

第十二课 茶馆和星巴克
Lesson 12 Teahouse and Starbucks

　　观察和了解中国文化的最好方式之一，就是去中国的茶馆坐坐。在茶馆里，你不仅可以听到人们对政治经济和日常生活的评论，也可以欣赏到中国的传统艺术。在一千三百年前的唐朝，中国就出现了茶馆。起初，茶馆是文学家、诗人和艺术家讨论问题，交流思想的地方，以后才慢慢地成为普通百姓聊天休息、会晤朋友的场所。

　　中国各地茶馆的特点也是不同的，比如北京、杭州、成都和广州的茶馆。北京的茶馆里有时会有京剧和相声表演；杭州的茶馆会有评弹表演；成都的茶馆里一般都会设有麻将桌；而广州的茶馆里，还会供应大量的食品，被称为茶餐。茶馆也是商人们进行商务会谈时经常选择的地方。中国是茶的故乡，茶文化和茶艺表演是中国民俗文化的重要组成部分。

第十二课 茶馆和星巴克
Lesson 12 Teahouse and Starbucks

　　像中国人喜欢喝茶一样,很多美国人喜欢喝咖啡,咖啡屋也就成了美国人休闲的主要场所。总部位于西雅图的星巴克咖啡,因其别具特色的咖啡产品和全球性的经营模式,成为美国咖啡休闲的主要代表。

　　与中国的茶馆不同,星巴克的早晨特别繁忙。很多上班或上学的人在这里吃早餐。顾客没时间坐下来吃,就通过汽车购物窗口买,然后边开车边吃。来星巴克休闲的人也不少,他们或者看书读报,或者聊天谈事。但在星巴克里是不会像中国茶馆那样进行艺术表演的,也许大家认为艺术表演更应该在酒吧里,而不是在咖啡屋里。星巴克的收银付货速度很快,充分表现出了美国快节奏的商业休闲文化特征。

评论 pínglùn	comment		麻将 májiàng	mahjong
欣赏 xīnshǎng	appreciate		供应 gōngyìng	supply
起初 qǐchū	in the beginning		民俗 mínsú	folklore
文学家 wénxuéjiā	literateur		别具特色 bié jù tèsè	with special characteristics
诗人 shīrén	poet		全球性 quánqiúxìng	globalization
思想 sīxiǎng	thought		模式 móshì	mode
百姓 bǎixìng	common people		繁忙 fánmáng	busy
聊天 liáotiān	gossip		顾客 gùkè	customer
会晤 huìwù	meet, contact		收银 shōuyín	cashier
京剧 jīngjù	Beijing opera		付货 fù huò	deliver commodity
相声 xiàngshēng	cross talk, comic dialogue		速度 sùdù	speed
评弹 píngtán	Ping Tan		节奏 jiézòu	pace, rhythm

专有名词 Proper Nouns

唐朝 Tángcháo	Tang Dynasty		广州 Guǎngzhōu	a city of China
成都 Chéngdū	a city of China		西雅图 Xīyǎtú	Seattle

课文理解 Understanding of the Text

一、判 断 True-false questions

1. 去茶馆是了解中国文化的好办法之一。　　　　　□ 对　□ 错
2. 中国的茶馆已经有一百多年的历史了。　　　　　□ 对　□ 错
3. 北京、杭州、成都和广州的茶馆都差不多。　　　□ 对　□ 错
4. 茶文化和茶艺表演是中国民俗文化的重要组成部分。□ 对　□ 错
5. 在经营方式上，星巴克和中国茶馆一样。　　　　□ 对　□ 错

二、选 择 Multiple choice

1. 中国的茶馆出现在_____年前。
   A. 1100　　　　B. 1200　　　　C. 1300　　　　D. 1400
2. 最初，茶馆是_____讨论艺术，交流思想的地方。
   A. 工人　　　　B. 农民　　　　C. 艺术家　　　D. 商人
3. 北京的茶馆有_____，杭州的茶馆有_____，成都的茶馆有_____，而广州的茶馆有_____。
   A. 京剧和相声表演　B. 麻将　　　　C. 评弹表演　　D. 很多食品
4. _____是茶的故乡。
   A. 日本　　　　B. 中国　　　　C. 美国　　　　D. 墨西哥
5. 中国茶馆和星巴克咖啡都属于_____文化。
   A. 古代　　　　B. 体育　　　　C. 休闲　　　　D. 服装

三、问 答 Short answer questions

1. 中国各地的茶馆有什么不同？
   What differences are there in the tea houses in each region of China?
2. 星巴克咖啡和中国茶馆在经营上有什么不同？
   What's the difference between Starbucks and Chinese teahouse in running aspect?

http://www.09987.com/
http://www.gdsmart.net/
http://www.cluyu.cn/
http://www.teabs.com/
http://www.beiguicoffee.com/
http://www.coffee-in-china.com/
http://www.coffeeb2b.com/index.html
http://chineseteas101.com/
http://www.chinavista.com/experience/tea/tea.html
http://chinese-tea.net/
http://www.travelchinaguide.com/
http://www.starbucks.com/
http://www.coffeeresearch.org/
http://www.ineedcoffee.com/08/chinese-coffee/
http://www.streetdirectory.com/
http://www.teanobi.com/
http://www.o-cha.com/
http://www.holymtn.com/

绿茶 Green tea

汉语拼音_____

第十二课 茶馆和星巴克
Lesson 12 Teahouse and Starbucks

花茶 Floral tea

汉语拼音_____

乌龙茶 Oolong tea

汉语拼音_____

功夫茶 Kongfu tea

汉语拼音_____

酥油茶 Butter tea

汉语拼音_____

拓展活动
Extention

一、探索 Exploration

1. 观摩一次中国茶艺表演。
   Appreciate Chinese tea ceremony.

2. 通过下列图片谈谈中国茶艺和日本茶道的不同，并简述一下日本茶道的历史：
   By the pictures below, what is the difference between the tea ceremony of China and the tea ceremony of Japan? Briefly introduce the history of the Japanese tea ceremony:

二、讨论 Discussion

中国和美国休闲文化的异同。
The difference between the leisure culture of China and the United States.

三、报告 Presentation

1. 茶文化是怎样传播到西方的？咖啡文化是怎样传播到中国的？
   How was the tea culture spread to the Western counteies, and how was the coffee culture spread to China?
2. 最近十年中国咖啡消费概况。
   The coffee consumption of the last ten years in China.

Going to a Chinese tea house Is the one of the best ways to observe and understand Chinese culture. In a tea house, not only will you hear how people discuss politics, economy and daily life, but also you will appreciate Chinese traditional art. Tea houses appeared in China 1,300 years ago, during the Tang Dynasty. In the beginning, the tea house was a place for literateurs, poets and artists to discuss their work and communicate, and then it became the place for common people to gossip, rest and meet with friends.

The features of tea houses are different in each region of China. Take the tea houses in Beijing, Hangzhou, Chengdu and Guangzhou for example. There is a performance of Beijing opera or cross talk in Beijing's tea house, "Ping Tan"—a musical storytelling show in Hangzhou's tea house, mahjong in Chengdu's tea house, and many food options in Guangzhou's tea house, called tea cuisine. The tea house is a typical choice for businessmen to go to, to talk about their affairs. China is the home of tea; tea culture and tea ceremony is an important component of Chinese folklore.

Just as Chinese prefer drinking tea, lots of Americans prefer drinking coffee. The coffee shop is a main place for Americans to spend their leisure time. Starbucks, with its headquarter in Seattle, is an important representative of coffee culture of the United States because of her featured coffee products and global management.

Unlike the Chinese tea house, it is very busy in the morning at Starbucks. Many people who go to work and school have their breakfast there. If in a hurry, a customer will order by drive-thru, and have his breakfast while driving. There are many people who spend their spare time at Starbucks; they read or talk. But Starbucks will not hold performances as a Chinese tea house does; it is more likely that a performance will be in a bar, not a coffee shop. Starbucks cashiers work very fast; this sufficiently presents the high speed commercial leisure culture.

第十三课　乒乓球和棒球
Pīngpāngqiú hé bàngqiú

Lesson 13 *Pingpong and Baseball*

　　乒乓球运动虽然起源于英国，但它是中国的"国球"。其中很大的一个原因是，1959年4月，中国乒乓球运动员容国团 (Róng Guótuán, Mr. Rong Guotuan) 在德国为中华人民共和国赢得了第一个世界冠军，这也是中国自清朝以来获得的第一个现代竞技运动项目的冠军。从此以后，乒乓球运动在中国迅速普及，成为了中国的"国球"。

　　乒乓球运动投资少，设备简单，并且具有适于东方人身材矮小灵活，反应迅速的特点，这也是乒乓球运动能够在中国首先发展的原因之一。20世纪80年代以后，除乒乓球外，其他运动项目在中国发展也很快，羽毛球、体操、跳水、举重等项目上也获得了很多世界冠军。虽然如此，中国人仍然认为乒乓球是中国的"国球"。

棒球、橄榄球和篮球这三个运动项目被称为美国的"国球"。有人认为棒球起源于英国的板球，但它与板球有很大的不同。亚历山大·卡特来特(Yàlìshāndà Kǎtèláitè, Mr. Alexander Cartwright)是美国棒球规则的第一个制定者，我们可以认为棒球是美国特有的运动项目之一。

　　棒球是一项集体项目，与乒乓球相比，装备比较昂贵，并且需要比较大的场地。很多美国人特别喜爱棒球运动。到了职业联赛的季节，球场里更是热闹非凡。但由于棒球在国际上缺乏普及性，2008年北京奥运会时，被列为表演项目，而在2012年伦敦奥运会上，则将取消这个项目。但无论怎样，棒球在美国人的心目中，永远是他们所喜爱的"国球"之一。

词汇 Vocabulary

冠军 guànjūn	champion	跳水 tiàoshuǐ	dive
以来 yǐlái	since	举重 jǔzhòng	weight lifting
现代 xiàndài	modern	橄榄球 gǎnlǎnqiú	American football; rugby
竞技 jìngjì	sports, athletics	篮球 lánqiú	basketball
运动 yùndòng	sport	板球 bǎnqiú	cricket
项目 xiàngmù	item	规则 guīzé	rule
迅速 xùnsù	fast, quickly	制定 zhìdìng	constitute, establish, set down
投资 tóuzī	investment	装备 zhuāngbèi	equipment equipment; furnishment
设备 shèbèi	equipment	昂贵 ángguì	expensive
身材 shēncái	stature	职业联赛 zhíyè liánsài	professional league
矮小 ǎixiǎo	short (body)	季节 jìjié	season
灵活 línghuó	agility	非凡 fēifán	uncommon
反应 fǎnyìng	reflect	国际 guójì	international
羽毛球 yǔmáoqiú	badminton	无论 wúlùn	no matter, whatever
体操 tǐcāo	gymnastics		

专有名词 Proper Nouns

英国 Yīngguó	United Kingdom of Great Britain
德国 Déguó	Germany
中华人民共和国 Zhōnghuá Rénmín Gònghéguó	People's Republic of China

奥运会 Àoyùnhuì	Olympic Games
伦敦 Lúndūn	London

课文理解 Understanding of the Text

一、判断 True-false questions

1. 乒乓球起源于中国，所以是中国的"国球"。　　□ 对　□ 错
2. 1959年四月，李小龙（Bruce Lee）在美国为中国取得了第一个乒乓球世界冠军。　　□ 对　□ 错
3. 乒乓球运动投资少，设备简单。　　□ 对　□ 错
4. 棒球装备比较昂贵，并需要比较大的场地。　　□ 对　□ 错
5. 棒球也是中国的"国球"之一。　　□ 对　□ 错

二、选择 Multiple choice

1. 中国的"国球"是_____。
   A. 羽毛球　　B. 乒乓球　　C. 棒球　　D. 橄榄球
2. 乒乓球运动起源于_____。
   A. 美国　　B. 英国　　C. 中国　　D. 德国
3. 乒乓球在中国首先发展的原因不包括_____。
   A. 投资少　　B. 设备简单　　C. 适合东方人特点　　D. 场地较大
4. 美国的"国球"是_____。
   A. 棒球　　B. 篮球　　C. 乒乓球　　D. 橄榄球

5. _____ 年伦敦奥运会将不再进行棒球比赛。

A. 2008　　　B. 2012　　　C. 2016　　　D. 2020

三、问 答 Short answer questions

1. 为什么说乒乓球是中国的"国球"？

   Why is Pingpong a Chinese national sport?

2. 为什么说棒球是美国的"国球"之一？

   Why is it said that baseball is one of the national sports of the United States?

http://www.cycnet.com/encyclopedia/sport/histor/chinasport/
http://www.56-china.com.cn/
http://www.chinasportstoday.com/en/
http://www.travelchinaguide.com/intro/focus/sport.htm
http://www.wushu.com.cn/
http://www.72so.net/
http://dragonboat.sport.org.cn/
http://www.taichi-arts.com/
http://www.yijiaowushu.com/
http://www.sfwushu.net/
http://www.bostondragonboat.org/
http://www.bostondragonboat.org/
http://www.clubxiangqi.com/
http://www.chessvariants.com/xiangqi.html
http://www.chess.com/
http://www.uschess.org/
http://www.chessclub.com/
http://www.shuttlecock-usa.org/
http://www.goodorient.com/Chinese_Jianzi
http://www.mzb.com.cn/
http://wikitravel.org/en/Xinjiang
http://www.truexinjiang.com/
http://www.paulnoll.com/China/Minorities/min-Kazakh.html

武术 Martial arts, Wushu

汉语拼音＿＿＿＿＿＿＿＿＿＿＿＿＿＿＿＿＿＿＿＿＿＿＿＿＿＿

气功 Qigong

汉语拼音＿＿＿＿＿＿＿＿＿＿＿＿＿＿＿＿＿＿＿＿＿＿＿＿＿＿

叼羊 Sheep-snatching

汉语拼音＿＿＿＿＿＿＿＿＿＿＿＿＿＿＿＿＿＿＿＿＿＿＿＿＿＿

第十三课 乒乓球和棒球
Lesson 13 Pingpong and Baseball

赛牦牛 Yak Race

汉语拼音_____

赛龙舟 Dragon-boat Race

汉语拼音_____

太极拳 Shadowboxing, Tai-chi Boxer

汉语拼音_____

一、探索 Exploration

踢毽子是中国民间传统运动项目之一。它起源于1800年前的中国。踢毽子的规则很简单，主要用脚踢，也可使用身体其他部位做出各种花样和技术动作，但不能用手触摸或辅助。如毽子落地，即为失败。毽子的制作方法也很简单，方法是：先将动物的尾羽捆扎成束，插入作为底托的带孔重物中，再用布裹紧缝牢即可。请做几个毽子，然后踢踢看。

Kicking shuttlecock is one of the Chinese traditional folk sports. It originated in China 1,800 years ago. The rule of kicking shuttlecock is very simple. A person kicks with his feet mainly. The other parts of body can be used to make various figured and skilled actions. However, it is forbidden to use hands. If the shuttlecock falls to the ground, the player(s) fails. It is quite easy to make a shuttlecock. The method is, first, to pack tail feather of animals into a bundle, and then plug it with a heavy thing with a hole as a button of the shuttlecock. Finally, wrap it with a piece of cloth and sew it firmly. Please make some shuttlecocks and try playing with them.

二、讨论 Discussion

先了解一下中国象棋和国际象棋的规则，然后讨论从不同的规则中反映出来的中西文化的不同。

Please learn the rules of Chinese chess and Western chess first, and then talk about the difference between Chinese culture and Western culture based on the rules.

三、报告 Presentation

2008年北京奥运会对中国及世界其他国家的影响。
The influence of the 2008 Olympics in Beijing, China on China and the rest of the world.

Pingpong is a Chinese national sport, although it came from England. One important reason is that Chinese Pingpong player, Mr. Rong Guotuan, in Germany, won the first world championship for the People's Republic of China in April 1959; this is also the first championship that China won in modern athletics since the Qing dynasty. Pingpong has been popularized since that time, and has become the national sport of China.

Another reason why Pingpong could be developed first in China is that there is less investment involved and simple equipment, as well as that it fits an Easterner's short and agile body. Since the 1980s, other sports have developed quickly in China also; the Chinese also won lots of world championships in badminton, gymnastics, diving, weight-lifting and more. Nevertheless, the Chinese people still consider Pingpong as their national sport.

Baseball, football and basketball are called the national sports is the United States. It is said that baseball originated from cricket of England, but they are much different. Mr. Alexander Cartwright wrote the first rules of baseball in the United States. Therefore, we see that baseball is really an American sport.

Baseball is a kind of collective sport. Compared with Pingpong, the furnishment is rather expensive and the field is required to be larger. Many Americans are fond of baseball. During the season of Major League, the stadiums are full of uncommon liveliness. Because of lacking worldwide popularity, baseball was only a performance item in the Beijing Olympic Games in 2008 and it will be cancelled in the London Olympic Games in 2012. No matter what happens, baseball is always the national sport for American people.

第十四课 出发
Lesson 14 Let's Go!

中国和美国都是旅游大国，但两国的旅游项目各有特色。中国的旅游项目可以分为自然景观旅游、人文景观旅游和民族风情旅游三大类型。比如黄山、九寨沟、张家界等景区属于自然景观旅游；北京故宫、西安兵马俑属于人文景观旅游；云南大理、西藏拉萨则属于民族风情旅游。另外也有像杭州西湖和北京长城、颐和园那样的融自然景观旅游和人文景观旅游为一体的旅游类型。

中国历史漫长，文物古迹很多，所以在旅游时，建议游客到一个景点之前，先了解一下那个景点的历史，这样旅游起来才更有意思。如果你到中国的首都北京，那里的"胡同风情游"很有特点，它能让你体验北京的历史和老百姓的生活。

（左）黄山
（右）兵马俑

（左）布达拉宫(Potala)
（右）西湖

在美国的旅游类型中，除了自然景观旅游和人文景观旅游外，"知识旅游"是一项在中国旅游中不太常见的旅游项目。它反映出了美国作为一个年轻的国家在文化上的特殊魅力。作为世界上最大的移民国家和最先进的工业化国家，除博物馆外，参观美国世界顶级的企业和大学也都成为了旅游项目。比如，西雅图的波音 (Bōyīn, Boeing) 飞机公司、休斯顿 (Xiūsīdùn, Houston) 的宇航中心、宾夕法尼亚 (Bīnxīfǎníyà, Pennsylvania) 州的赫尔西 (Hè'ěrxī, Hershey's) 巧克力公司、加利福尼亚 (Jiālìfúníyà, California) 的斯坦福大学 (Sītǎnfú Dàxué, Stanford University)、麻省理工学院 (Máshěng Lǐgōng Xuéyuàn, MIT) 都是旅行社经常推荐游客去参观的景点。

由此可见，国情不同，文化不同，旅游项目也有所不同。因此，在你出发之前，一定要具备一些比较文化学的知识。

波音飞机博物馆

麻省理工学院

词汇 Vocabulary

旅游 lǚyóu	tour, journey		胡同 hútòng	alley, bystreet
自然 zìrán	nature		体验 tǐyàn	experience
景观 jǐngguān	scenery		知识 zhīshi	knowledge
人文 rénwén	humanity		反映 fǎnyìng	reflect
风情 fēngqíng	folk		魅力 mèilì	fascination
融……为…… róng……wéi……	blend, melt, compromise		先进 xiānjìn	advanced
漫长 màncháng	long		顶级 dǐngjí	top level
文物 wénwù	cultural relic		企业 qǐyè	enterprise
古迹 gǔjì	historical site		宇航 yǔháng	space navigation
建议 jiànyì	suggest		巧克力 qiǎokèlì	chocolate
游客 yóukè	tourist, visitor		推荐 tuījiàn	recommend
景点 jǐngdiǎn	view spot		具备 jùbèi	have, process

专有名词 Proper Nouns

黄山 Huáng Shān	Mt. Huang Shan		张家界 Zhāngjiājiè	a view spot in Hunan Prouince
九寨沟 Jiǔzhàigōu	a view spot in Sichuan Prouince		西安 Xī'ān	a city of China

兵马俑 Bīngmǎyǒng	Terra Cotta Warriors and Horses	拉萨 Lāsà	Lhasa
云南 Yúnnán	a province of China	西湖 Xī Hú	West Lake, Xi Hu
大理 Dàlǐ	a city in Yunnan province	长城 Chángchéng	the Great Wall
西藏 Xīzàng	Tibet	颐和园 Yíhé Yuán	the Summer Palace

课文理解 Understanding of the Text

一、判断 True-false questions

1. 中国和美国都是旅游大国，但两国的旅游项目各有特色。☐ 对 ☐ 错
2. 黄山、九寨沟、张家界等景区属于人文景观旅游。☐ 对 ☐ 错
3. 云南大理、西藏拉萨属于民族风情旅游。☐ 对 ☐ 错
4. 西安的"胡同风情游"很有意思。☐ 对 ☐ 错
5. 知识旅游是美国旅游的一大特色。☐ 对 ☐ 错

二、选择 Multiple choice

1. 中国旅游的三大类型是 _____，_____，和 _____。
   A. 人文景观旅游　B. 自然景观旅游　C. 知识旅游　D. 民族风情旅游
2. 黄山和张家界属于_____。
   A. 人文景观旅游　B. 自然景观旅游　C. 知识旅游　D. 民族风情旅游
3. 云南大理和西藏拉萨属于_____。
   A. 人文景观旅游　B. 自然景观旅游　C. 知识旅游　D. 民族风情旅游
4. 北京的_____是很有特色的旅游项目。
   A. 人文景观旅游　B. 自然景观旅游　C. 胡同风情游　D. 民族风情旅游
5. 游览斯坦福大学属于_____。
   A. 人文景观旅游　B. 自然景观旅游　C. 知识旅游　D. 民族风情旅游

三、问答 Short answer questions

1. 中国旅游的主要类型是什么？
   What are the main types of tourism in China?
2. 美国旅游的主要类型是什么？
   What are the main types of tourism in United States?

http://www.51yala.com/
http://www.china.travel/
http://www.cncn.com/
http://www.xbly365.com/
http://www.chinatour.com/
http://www.chinese-tools.com/travel
http://www.goingtochina.com/
http://chinesefestival.org/
http://www.chinapage.com/festival/festival.html
http://www.chinahighlights.com/travelguide/festivals/
http://bjhutong.abang.com/
http://www.beijingtraveltips.com/
http://www.beijingpage.com/
http://www.shanghaihighlights.com/
http://www.travelchinaguide.com/cityguides/shanghai.htm
http://www.shanghaitour.net/
http://www.bjlyw.com/
http://www.expo2010.cn/
http://en.expo2010.cn/

长城 The Great Wall

汉语拼音_____

那达慕 Naddam

汉语拼音_____

丝绸之路 The Silk Road

汉语拼音_____

茶马古道 The Ancient Tea-Horse Trade Road

汉语拼音_____

黄帝陵 The Huangdi Tomb

汉语拼音_____

拓展活动 Extention

一、探索 Exploration

北京"胡同风情游"都有哪些活动内容？
What are the activities of Beijing Alley Folk Tour?

二、讨论 Discussion

中国"民族风情游"与美国"印第安人保留区旅游"的异同。
The difference between Chinese minorities folk tourism and Indian Reservation tourism in the United States.

三、报告 Presentation

请你拟定一个三天的上海旅游方案，并填写下列表格：
Please make out a three-day Shanghai tourism plan and fill in the form below:

时 间 Time	活动内容 Activities	理 由 Reasons	准备工作 Preparation
第一天上午 Morning of 1st day			
第一天中午 Noon of 1st day			
第一天下午 Afternoon of 1st day			
第一天晚上 Evening of 1st day			
第二天上午 Morning of 2nd day			
第二天中午 Noon of 2nd day			
第二天下午 Afternoon of 2nd day			
第二天晚上 Evening of 2nd day			
第三天上午 Morning of 3rd day			
第三天中午 Noon of 3rd day			
第三天下午 Afternoon of 3rd day			
第三天晚上 Evening of 3rd day			

英语译文
English Version of the Text

Both China and the United States are important countries for tourism, but each has her own features that attract tourists. There are three types of tourism in China: natural scenery tourism, humanity scenery tourism and minorities folk tourism. For example, the view spots of Mt. Huang Shan, Jiu Zhai Gou, Zhang Jia Jie are natural scenery tourism, the Palace Museum in Beijing, Terra Cotta Warriors and Horses in Xi'an are humanity scenery tourism, and Dali in Yunnan, and Lhasa in Tibet are minorities folk tourism. Additionally, the West Lake in Hangzhou and the Great Wall and the Summer Palace in Beijing are an integration of natural scenery tourism and humanity scenery tourism.

China has a long history, and lots of cultural relics and historical sites. Therefore, it is advised to read some information about the view spots before visiting; this will make your tour more meaningful. If you are in Beijing, the capital of China, the Alley Folk Tour is very interesting; it will allow you to experience the history of Beijing and daily life of the common people there.

Educational tourism is a tourism type in the United States which is hardly found in China. However, the United States, like China, has natural scenery tourism and humanity scenery tourism. Educational tourism reflects the special cultural fascination of the United States as a young country. As the biggest immigration country, and the most advanced industrial country, besides the museums, visiting the top-level enterprises and universities worldwide are all the tour items. For example, Boeing in Seattle, the Space Center in Houston, Hershey's in Pennsylvania, Stanford University in California, and MIT in Massachusetts are the view spots usually recommended by travel agents.

It is found, therefore, that the tour items of the United States and China are different by the different national conditions and culture. So before starting to tour China, you should have some information about the comparative culturology.

第十五课　商店趣事
Lesson 15 Funny Stories in the Store

　　中国在20世纪的50到70年代，由于实行计划经济和长期的政治运动，使得经济在有些方面发展很慢。那时候，商店里的东西也比较少，人们买东西经常要排长队。所以，只要商店里一排长队，就有可能是在卖什么好的或便宜的东西。有一个笑话说，一个未婚的小伙子看见又在排长队了，看也不看一下，就排上队了，排到了才知道是在卖姑娘化妆用的口红。

北京中关村商业街

现在的中国,商店里的商品十分丰富,各种质量,各种价位的都有。商店也特别多,人们购物十分方便。要是买食品和一般生活必需品的话,那就更方便了。所以中国人买食品时,一般一次不会买很多,因为商店离家很近,随时都可以买,保证吃到新鲜的食品。不过,最近几年,由于经济的快速发展和工资的提高,物价要比以前高了很多。

美国的商店与中国的相比有两个最大的不同之处。一个是,无论你走到美国的哪个州,都会发现很多商店的名字是相同的。比如QFC、赛富威(Sàifùwēi, Safeway)、弗雷梅尔(Fúléiméi'ěr, Fred Myer)、克斯克(Kèsīkè, Costco)、沃尔玛(Wò'ěrmǎ, Walmart)、JC便士(JC Biànshì, JC Penny)。不但名字相同,出售的商品和价格也好像差不多,这是因为美国的零售业是被这些大零售企业控制的。另一个是,与中国人相比,美国人买食品一次会买很多,一般来讲,起码是可以用上一个星期,甚至一个月的。这个情况大概跟美国的商业网点不太密集有关。

无论美国的商店还是中国的商店,到了节日和假日的时候,都会减价打折。到了那个时候,商店里特别热闹。

(左)华盛顿州的一家沃尔玛

(右)北京的一家沃尔玛

词汇 Vocabulary

中文	英文	中文	英文
实行 shíxíng	carry out, implement	保证 bǎozhèng	assure, guarantee
计划经济 jìhuà jīngjì	planned economy	新鲜 xīnxiān	fresh
笑话 xiàohua	joke	物价 wùjià	price
未婚 wèihūn	single, unmarried	差不多 chàbuduō	almost, nearly
化妆 huàzhuāng	dressing, make up	零售业 língshòuyè	retail trade
口红 kǒuhóng	lipstick	起码 qǐmǎ	at least
质量 zhìliàng	quality	密集 mìjí	dense, compression
价位 jiàwèi	price	减价 jiǎn jià	mark down, cheapen
生活必需品 shēnghuó bìxūpǐn	necessity for daily life	打折 dǎ zhé	discount, rebate
随时 suíshí	at any time, momentarily		

课文理解 Understanding of the Text

一、判断 True-false questions

1. 中国在20世纪的50年代到70年代实行计划经济政策。 □对 □错
2. 笑话里说，那个小伙子最后才知道他排队买的是牙刷。 □对 □错
3. 现在的中国，商店里商品十分丰富。 □对 □错
4. 最近几年，中国由于经济的变化和工资的提高，
   物价要比以前高了很多。 □对 □错
5. 克斯克和沃尔玛是中国的商店。 □对 □错

二、选择 Multiple choice

1. 中国在20世纪的50年代到70年代，商店里的商品很少，这是因为_____和_____。
   A. 战争　　　B. 计划经济　　C. 政治运动　　D. 地震

2. 中国人买食品一次不会买很多，这是因为_____。
   A. 商店离家比较近　　　　B. 不新鲜
   C. 没钱　　　　　　　　　D. 商品太少

3. 最近几年，由于_____的快速发展和_____的提高，物价要比以前高了很多。
   A. 政治　　　B. 工资　　　C. 经济　　　D. 商品

4. 美国人买食品一次就会买很多，这个情况大概跟美国的商业网点_____有关。
   A. 十分密集　　B. 不太密集

5. 到了节日的时候，中国和美国的商店都_____。
   A. 减价　　　B. 涨价

三、问答 Short answer questions

1. 为什么说那个小伙子的故事是个笑话？
   Why is the story of that chap a joke?

2. 中国人购物和美国人有什么不同之处？
   What is the difference between China and United States in shopping?

http://www.zhlzh.com/
http://www.chinahighlights.com/beijing/shopping.htm
http://www.orientaltravel.com/
http://www.yishu999.com/
http://www.shchm.org/
http://www.njfzm.com/

http://tibet.mjjq.com/4313.html
http://d.lotour.com/guojidabazha/
http://www.qyc.com.cn/
http://www.pikeplacemarket.org/frameset.asp?flash=false
http://www.mcdonalds.com/
http://www.kfc.com/
http://www.walmart.com/
http://www.lingshou.com/
http://chinese-school.netfirms.com/businessculture.html
http://www.cyborlink.com/besite/china.htm
http://www.chinese-culture.net/html/chinese_business_culture.html
http://www.silkstreet.cc/templet/default/
http://www.beijingtraveltips.com/shopping/xiu_shui/xiushui.htm
http://www.ebeijing.gov.cn/feature_2/hsib/shop/t1009120.htm

资料搜集 / Data Collection

北京琉璃厂 Beijing Color Glaze Plant Street, Liu Li Chang

汉语拼音_____

上海城隍庙 The Temple of the Town Guardian Angel of Shanghai, Cheng Huang Temple

汉语拼音_____

第十五课 商店趣事
Lesson 15 Funny Stories in the Store

南京夫子庙 Nanjing Confucius Temple, Fu Zi Miao Temple

汉语拼音_____

拉萨八角街 Barkhor Street of Lhasa, Ba Jiao Jie Street

汉语拼音_____

乌鲁木齐国家大巴扎 Urumqi Great International Bazaar

汉语拼音_____

天津劝业场 Quan Ye Chang, Tianjin

汉语拼音_____

一、探索 Exploration

请解释北京秀水街形成的原因。
Please comment on the reason why Beijing Xiu Shui Jie Street formed.

二、讨论 Discussion

1. 中国是市场经济国家吗？
   Is China a market economy country?
2. 中国传统文化对商业文化的影响。
   How does Chinese traditional culture impact the commercial culture?

三、报告 Presentation

中国文化对麦当劳、肯德基、苹果、沃尔玛在华企业的影响。
How does Chinese traditional culture impact the enterprises of McDonalds, Kentucky Fried Chicken, Macintosh, and Walmart located in China?

English Version of the Text

From the 1950s to the 1970s, the economy grew slowly in some aspects in China because of the planned economy and the long-period political movements. At that time, there were few commodities in the store and people had to stand in a long line to purchase them. Once there was a long line in a store, there was probably something good or cheap for sale. A joke says an unmarried chap found a long line and he stood in it without even asking what was for sale. He didn't realize the line was for girl's lipstick until it was his turn to buy.

In current China, a store has rich and various commodities in a variety of quality and price. The stores are so numerous that people go shopping conveniently. If one only wants food and daily life necessities, it is much more convenient. That's why Chinese won't buy lots of food for one time generally, because the store is near their house, and they can buy it at any time to assure they can have fresh food. But in recent years, with the rapid economic development and the rise of salary, the prices of commodities are much higher than before.

There are two differences between China and the United States. One is that no matter which state you visit, you will find many stores have the same name, for example, QFC, Safeway, Fred Meyer, Costco, Walmart, JC Penney, and so on. Not only do they have the same names, but the commodities they are selling and the price are almost the same; this is because the retail trade is controlled by these retail companies. The other difference is, compared with the Chinese, Americans will buy lots of things at one time, generally, which are enough for one week at least, even for one month. This relates probably to the lack of a large commercial outlets.

Whether in China or in the United States, stores always offer a big sale during festivals and holidays. During this time, stores are very noisy.

部分练习答案
Keys to Exercises

第一课 Lesson 1

一、判断
1. 错　　2. 对　　3. 错　　4. 错　　5. 对

二、选择
1. A D　　2. C　　3. A C　　4. B D　　5. C

第二课 Lesson 2

一、判断
1. 对　　2. 错　　3. 对　　4. 对　　5. 错

二、选择
1. B　　2. B C　　3. E　　4. D　　5. B

第三课 Lesson 3

一、判断
1. 错　　2. 错　　3. 对　　4. 错　　5. 对

二、选择
1. CBDA　　2. ABBA　　3. C　　4. C　　5. C

第四课 Lesson 4

一、判断
1. 对　　2. 错　　3. 错　　4. 对　　5. 错

二、选择
1. C　　2. C　　3. B　　4. DB　　5. B

第五课 Lesson 5

一、判断
1. 错　　2. 对　　3. 错　　4. 对　　5. 对

二、选择
   1. C   2. C   3. B   4. C   5. B

第六课　Lesson 6

一、判断
   1. 错   2. 错   3. 对   4. 对   5. 对
二、选择
   1. D B   2. C   3. A   4. B A   5. D

第七课　Lesson 7

一、判断
   1. 错   2. 对   3. 对   4. 错   5. 对
二、选择
   1. B   2. C   3. D   4. A   5. AC

第八课　Lesson 8

一、判断
   1. 错   2. 对   3. 错   4. 对   5. 错
二、选择
   1. A   2. BC   3. C   4. D   5. BD

第九课　Lesson 9

一、判断
   1. 错   2. 对   3. 对   4. 错   5. 对
二、选择
   1. C   2. AB   3. C   4. B   5. C

第十课　Lesson 10

一、判断
   1. 错   2. 错   3. 对   4. 对   5. 错

二、选择
1. C 2. BA 3. B 4. C 5. B

第十一课 Lesson 11

一、判断
1. 对 2. 错 3. 对 4. 对 5. 错

二、选择
1. D 2. C 3. C 4. B 5. C

第十二课 Lesson 12

一、判断
1. 对 2. 错 3. 错 4. 对 5. 错

二、选择
1. C 2. C 3. ACBD 4. B 5. C

第十三课 Lesson 13

一、判断
1. 错 2. 错 3. 对 4. 对 5. 错

二、选择
1. B 2. B 3. D 4. ABD 5. B

第十四课 Lesson 14

一、判断
1. 对 2. 错 3. 对 4. 错 5. 对

二、选择
1. ABD 2. B 3. D 4. C 5. C

第十五课 Lesson 15

一、判断
1. 对 2. 错 3. 对 4. 对 5. 错

二、选择
1. BC 2. A 3. CB 4. B 5. A

词汇总表
Vocabulary

A

矮小	13
按照	7
昂贵	13

B

百姓	12
班次	8
板球	13
办公	2
保险	10
保障	9
保证	15
奔驰	8
别具特色	12
濒临	1
病情	10
博物院(馆)	4
部	1

C

材料	7
采用	8
菜系	6
菜肴	6
草原	1
差距	9
差异	5
差不多	15
长寿	3
长途	8
程序	11
持续	9
充分	6
重建	4
出售	7
除……外	2
除非	8
传统	6
创造	3
刺激	11
从事	9
存在	5

D

答案	5
打招呼	5
打折	15
代表	3
贷款	7
担心	7
单调	6
单元	7
地点	2
地理	1
地区	1
地毯	1
电	7
顶级	14
对外	4

F

发源	6
发展	6
繁忙	12
反应	13
反映	14
方便	7
方言	5
非凡	13
分别	2
分餐制	11
丰盛	11
风景	1
风情	14
风味	6
封建	4
服务行业	9
付货	12
负担	9
复杂	11
副食	6

G

改革	10
盖房	7
橄榄球	13
个人所得税	9
根本	5
工具	8
公费	10

公寓	7
供应	12
共餐制	11
共同	3
贡献	9
沟通	5
购买	7
古迹	14
顾客	12
雇主	9
关系	3
关注	2
观察	8
观点	3
观念	3
官邸	4
官方	5
管理	2
冠军	13
广场	2
广阔	1
规则	13
国际	13
过程	10

H

海岸	1
含蓄	11
好转	10
和谐	11
后裔	3
胡同	14
互联网	10
化妆	15

还	7
环保	8
皇宫	4
皇权	4
黄牛党	10
会晤	12

J

几乎	5
机械	9
基本	4
级	1
急诊	10
计划经济	15
季节	13
既然	5
继承	6
继续	8
加工	6
家族	3
价位	15
减价	15
减轻	9
建议	14
建筑	4
健身	8
奖励	9
交通	8
角度	6
缴纳	9
缴税	9
节奏	12
结束	4
解决	10

金融	2
仅仅	3
京剧	12
经济	2
精美	4
精神	11
景点	14
景观	14
竞技	13
竞争	9
举重	13
具备	14
军队	4

K

开放	4
烤	6
口红	15
困扰	8

L

篮球	13
类似	7
类型	6
利润	9
联邦	2
辆	8
聊天	12
灵活	13
零售业	15
留心	8
流	1
楼梯	1
旅游	14

M

麻将	12
漫长	14
美丽	1
魅力	14
密集	15
民俗	12
民族自治区	2
明显	9
模式	12
目前	3

N

难怪	7
难免	10
内部	5
内向	11
农耕民族	6
农业	9

P

配合	11
烹饪	6
偏	10
频繁	9
品牌	6
平方	4
平均	9
平原	1
评弹	12
评论	12
普及	6
普通话	5

Q

其实	4
企业	14
起初	12
起码	15
气氛	11
气候	1
巧克力	14
亲戚	11
丘陵	1
全球性	12

R

染	4
热闹	11
人文	14
仍然	7
融……为……	14

S

沙漠	1
山峰	1
山脉	1
烧毁	4
少数	3
设备	13
设计	7
设计者	4
社会	3
社会福利	9
社区	10
身材	13
甚至	5
生活必需品	15
省	2
省会	2
诗人	12
实行	15
食材	6
世纪	8
收入	7
收银	12
手法	6
首都	2
首府	2
属于	10
说明	8
思想	12
速度	12
随处可见	6
随时	15
所有权	9

T

特别行政区	2
特色	5
体操	13
体验	14
跳水	13
通过	10
通宵	10
通用	5
投资	13
推荐	14

W

湾	1
……为主，……为辅	7
未婚	15
位置	3
文化	2

文物	14	医疗	10	整体	3
文学家	12	依据	9	政府	2
稳定	9	移民	3	政治	2
问题	3	以来	13	支付	7
无酒不成席	11	义务	9	支配	9
无论	13	音量	11	知识	14
物价	15	银行	7	直接	2
误解	3	隐私	11	值得	3

X

稀少	8	英尺	4	职务	9
先进	14	影响	1	职业联赛	13
现代	13	游客	14	职员	9
线路	8	游牧民族	6	制定	13
相当于	2	娱乐	11	制止	10
相对	8	与……相比	8	质量	15
相连	1	宇航	14	治好	10
想象	11	羽毛球	13	州	2
相声	12	语系	5	逐步	10
项目	13	语音	5	主人	4
象征	4	预约	10	主食	6
消除	5	元素	3	主体	3
笑话	15	园艺	6	主要	3
欣赏	12	院落	7	煮	6
新鲜	15	运动	13	助兴	11
性格	11	运河	1	注重	3
雄伟	4			著名	2
休闲	8	Z		专家	10
选定	4	增加	7	装备	13
迅速	13	宅基地	7	准	5

Y

宴请	11	占	3	自然	14
一般	2	招待	11	总统	4
一般来讲	2	招牌	11	租赁	7
		照顾	11	族群	3
		诊断	10		
		征收	9		

专有名词
Proper Nouns

A
奥运会	13

B
白宫	2
北京	1
兵马俑	14

C
长城	14
长江	1
成都	12
重庆	2

D
大理	14
大连	2
大西洋	1
大运河	1
傣族	6
德国	13

G
故宫	4
广东	5
广州	12

H
汉族	3
杭州	1

华盛顿	2
黄河	1
黄山	14

J
加拿大	1
九寨沟	14
旧金山	2

L
拉萨	14
伦敦	13
洛杉矶	2

M
蒙古族	6
明朝	4
墨西哥	1

N
纽约	2

O
欧洲	3

Q
青岛	2
清朝	4

S
上海	2
苏州	2

T
太平洋	1
唐朝	12
天津	2

W
维吾尔族	3

X
西安	14
西班牙	5
西藏	14
西湖	14
西雅图	12

Y
颐和园	14
英国	13
云南	14

Z
藏族	3
张家界	14
中华人民共和国	13
紫禁城	4